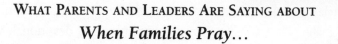
WHAT PARENTS AND LEADERS ARE SAYING ABOUT
When Families Pray...

"Cheri Fuller is a gifted mentor to today's Christian moms and dads. Warmly and insightfully, she helps us see what we want most for our families—and shows us how to make it happen."

DAVID KOPP
AUTHOR AND SENIOR EDITOR, *CHRISTIAN PARENTING TODAY*

"Cheri Fuller brings clarity and insight to simple stories of how prayer affects our everyday life. *When Families Pray* is a devotional book that will challenge every member of the family to believe God for the extraordinary. It is a must to have for your family!"

ALICE SMITH
INTERNATIONAL PRAYER COORDINATOR, U.S. PRAYER TRACK,
A.D. 2000 & BEYOND MOVEMENT

"In *When Families Pray*, Cheri Fuller skillfully crafts what some say can't be done—a sensitive devotional that reaches children, youth, and adults. Her warm, clever style facilitates intimate dialogue and prayer."

PAT VERBAL
FOUNDER, MINISTRY TO TODAY'S CHILD

"Cheri Fuller has done it again in giving us a 'blue ribbon' winner. This prayer book will enrich, encourage, help, and challenge us to pray more effectively. Practical and biblical!"

QUIN SHERRER
AUTHOR OF *HOW TO PRAY FOR YOUR CHILDREN*

"A grand slam by Cheri Fuller! *When Families Pray*, the third in the series, completes the cycle of encouraging, inspiring, and stimulating all members of the family to deepen their prayer life."

JILL HARRIS
INTERNATIONAL CHILDREN'S EXPO

"Cheri's format is varied, interesting, and creative. Family members of all ages will be blessed by her forthright emphasis on two relational components of meaningful prayer: observation and response."

BARBARA JAMES
DIRECTOR, WORLD INTERCESSION NETWORK

"Captivating real-life stories, practical ideas, plus wisdom from God's Word make *When Families Pray* a delightful family devotional. We are excited about using it with our own family as we continue discipling our four 'blessings' from God."

BOB AND DEBBY SJOGREN
(BOB) DIRECTOR, DESTINATION 2000
AUTHOR OF *UNVEILED AT LAST* AND *RUN WITH THE VISION*

"Each of these bite-size appetizers carries such an attractive, fresh-bread aroma that it can carry you beyond the book to the full meal of God's presence. *Bon appétit!*"

EMMETT COOPER, PH.D.
PRESIDENT, HONEYWORD® WAY OF LEARNING

"The biggest favor parents can do for their children is to introduce them to Jesus Christ and keep them in contact with Him through prayer. Teaching our kids to pray by example and apprenticeship is key. This book will provide the help parents need to accomplish this sacred task."

C. PETER WAGNER, PRESIDENT
DORIS M. WAGNER, EXECUTIVE DIRECTOR
GLOBAL HARVEST MINISTRIES

WHEN FAMILIES PRAY

ALSO BY CHERI FULLER

When Children Pray

When Mothers Pray

*Through the Learning Glass: A Child's Nine Learning Windows
You Don't Want to Miss*

Quiet Whispers from God's Heart for Women

Trading Your Worry for Wonder

21 Days to Helping Your Child Learn

Teaching Your Child to Write

Motherhood 101

Christmas Treasures of the Heart

Unlocking Your Child's Learning Potential

365 Ways to Develop Values in Your Child

365 Ways to Build Your Child's Self-Esteem

365 Ways to Help Your Child Learn and Achieve

How to Grow a Young Music Lover

Home Business Happiness

Helping Your Child Succeed in Public School

A Mother's Book of Wit and Wisdom

*Extraordinary Kids: Nurturing and Championing
Your Child with Special Needs*

CHERI FULLER

When Families Pray

Multnomah® Publishers *Sisters, Oregon*

WHEN FAMILIES PRAY
published by Multnomah Publishers, Inc.
and in association with the literary agency of Alive Communications, Inc.,
1465 Kelly Johnson Blvd., #320, Colorado Springs, CO 80920.

International Standard Book Number: 1-57673-412-9

Cover design by Kirk DouPonce
Cover photo by Tamara Reynolds Photography

Multnomah is a trademark of Multnomah Publishers, Inc., and is registered in the
U.S. Patent and Trademark Office.
The colophon is a trademark of Multnomah Publishers, Inc.

Printed in the United States of America

For information:
MULTNOMAH PUBLISHERS, INC.•P.O. BOX 1720•SISTERS, OR 97759

Library of Congress Cataloging-in-Publication Data
Fuller, Cheri.   When families pray/by Cheri Fuller.   p.cm.
    ISBN 1-57673-412-9 (alk. paper)
    1. Family Prayer—books and devotions—English. W. Devotional calendars. I. Title.
BV255.F79   1999   99-32885   CIP   249–dc21

99 00 01 02 03 04 05 06 — 10 9 8 7 6 5 4 3 2 1

ACKNOWLEDGMENTS

My grateful appreciation to those families who shared stories about God's marvelous answers to prayer, who love to pray, and who are developing in their kids a vision for the world, a love for God, and a love for prayer: especially Debby and Bob Sjogren, Cindy and Henry Smith, Pete Hohmann, Paula and Larry Dinkins, Jeff and Kristi Leeland, Dick Gruber, Bill Brown, the Wittman family, the Wingate family, and the Hemry family.

Many thanks from the bottom of my heart to my creative friend Connie Willems. Her research, insights, and skills helped this book come to life. A sincere thank you to my friend Marilyn Olson for typing assistance and support.

I'm grateful to Multnomah Publishers for their heart and vision for the importance of family prayer; to Greg Johnson, my agent; and to editors Dan Benson and Lisa Lauffer for the skills they brought to the project. And always, I thank my husband, Holmes, for his willingness to give grace at deadline time and for his love and prayers behind the scenes. My love and gratefulness to our children: Justin and wife Tiffany, Chris and wife Maggie, Alison, and precious Caitlin, our granddaughter. What a blessing it is to see the next generation love God and rise up as intercessors for their children, for the body of Christ, and for the world around them.

CONTENTS

How to Get
the Most from
When Families Pray

≋

If you've picked up this book, chances are you want to make prayer a priority in your family. And you probably understand that, while our children can learn about prayer at church, God has given parents the real responsibility—and privilege—of discipling our children in prayer.

Home is the perfect place for children to learn to talk with and listen to God, and to see such conversation modeled as a natural, daily habit. I've written *When Families Pray* to help you do just that. This book is a devotional designed to draw you and your children closer to each other and closer to God as you pray together. It provides a blueprint for a vital family prayer life and encourages you to develop the habit of prayer as you learn helpful concepts for praying effectively.

Each devotion in this book includes:

- A true story that both kids and parents can relate to (each story is a real-life event that is either documented in writing or has been personally related to me by a parent or Christian leader)
- A central Scripture

- Interactive "Discussion Openers" to stimulate sharing by all family members
- Scriptures for deeper study
- A suggested prayer that can inspire your own prayers
- A thought-provoking quote about prayer from a great thinker or author

As you and your children read aloud and discuss each devotion, you'll have the opportunity to learn many important principles of prayer: how understanding God's Father-love for us motivates us to pray; how as His children we have a direct line to God at all times; how we can give all our problems to Jesus; how our prayers impact others far away, even across the world; and much more.

You'll also discover some keys to effective prayer such as persevering, putting on God's armor, praying with childlike faith, praying Scripture, and forgiving enemies. And you'll read about and discuss some of the problems we face in prayer, such as when God answers our prayers with wait or even no.

This book has something for everyone in your family. There are stories your five-year-old will delight in and stories your older children will enjoy. You'll find accounts from history, from the Bible, from real-life families, and from some very real children. Reading these true stories aloud and discussing them will not only bond you as a family, they'll help you discover what God does when *your family* prays together!

As you make this discovery, you'll experience a wonderful opportunity to ask God about your family's special calling in the arena of prayer. In fact, you may feel overwhelmed at the possibilities! If you do, remember that God doesn't call us all to pray for everything everyday, but *He does call us to pray.* So as you read, choose and use the ideas or areas of prayer for which God gives your family a special passion.

Each devotion in this book also includes thought-provoking "Discussion Openers." You'll find simpler questions aimed at younger children and deeper questions to stimulate thought in your older kids and yourself. Use the questions to address your family's needs, adapting them as you see fit. If you have younger children, you might ask just one question or simply encourage them to discuss the story. If you have older children, you might encourage them to ask questions of their own. And if your kids don't immediately respond to the questions and discussion, don't lose hope. You never know when something will "click" and your children will realize an important truth. It can happen during family devotions or after "lights out" or while riding in the car.

To further encourage family prayer, you'll find sidebars with helpful prayer tips and creative, fun ways to apply specific stories to your own family. You'll read about one family that takes prayer drives and another that prays nightly for one of their "Christmas card families." You'll find helpful, creative suggestions for incorporating prayer into your daily schedule, such as having each child spin a globe after dinner and pray for the nation his or her finger lands on. Don't feel pressured to put all the ideas into practice (at least not all at the same time!). Instead, ask God what He has in store for your family.

So many parents tell me, "We have to teach our kids to pray! We don't want to let busyness keep us and our children from connecting with God, yet we have hectic schedules." That's why this book includes forty doable, bite-sized, and fun-to-read devotions that you can use in a variety of ways. You may want to devote eight weeks to prayer, reading one devotion every Monday through Friday. You may want to read just one or two devotions each week. Determine what works best for your family.

While these devotions are ideal for parents and children to enjoy together, grandparents or aunts and uncles may want to participate, too. You'll also find this book a helpful resource if you're a Sunday school teacher, children's church worker, or Christian school teacher. Whoever you are, you don't have to be a seasoned intercessor or a prayer scholar to benefit from this devotional or to help kids develop the habit of regular, personal communication with God.

I pray that this book will encourage you, inspire you, and help you point your children to their heavenly Father who desires to have ongoing communication with them throughout their whole lives. That's the major purpose of prayer! As Oswald Chambers said, "The end of prayer is that I will come to know God Himself." I also pray that as you walk through these devotions, God will knit your hearts together; that as you pray, you and your children will see Him work in new ways, sense His incredible faithfulness, and grow to trust Him more and more.

Your family will be blessed as you come together and pray. That's a promise because prayer is the key to blessing. And as your family prays not only for your own needs but for the needs of others, you'll receive the blessing first because you'll be touching God, the source of every grace, blessing, and gift (James 1:17).

May the Lord energize your family to be a blessing to others and mobilize you to join your prayers with other families and intercessors all over the world. Together, we can make an eternal difference in the lives of neighbors, families, friends, and even people groups and nations. The possibilities are endless when families pray!

Cheri Fuller

PRAYER JOURNAL
Your Family Prayer History

One of the best ways to build a spiritual heritage as a family is by recording your prayers and God's answers to those prayers. In Deuteronomy 6:7, God told the Israelites to remember and share with their children what He had done to protect, deliver, and provide for them. In the same way, God wants us to remember His wondrous acts in our lives. As we record them now and review them later, our hearts will fill with thanksgiving for the faithful God we serve. We will also be encouraged to trust Him in situations for which we do not yet see a ready answer.

Think of some of the most significant things God has done in your family and record them here. Then, as you read the devotions in this book and pray together, write new prayer requests and God's answers as they arise. By the time you've completed this book, you should have an entire history of God's faithfulness to your family. But I challenge you to continue this practice beyond the scope of this book—make it a lifelong habit to pray and acknowledge God's answers. Your faith will grow strong as you do!

DATE	NEED, REQUEST, OR PRAYER	GOD'S ANSWER

DATE	NEED, REQUEST, OR PRAYER	GOD'S ANSWER

DATE	NEED, REQUEST, OR PRAYER	GOD'S ANSWER

DATE	NEED, REQUEST, OR PRAYER	GOD'S ANSWER

ONE

Daddy Loves Me

≈

How great is the love the Father has lavished on us,
that we should be called children of God!

1 JOHN 3:1

raveling for work can be a lonely thing when you have to leave your family behind. When Bill travels, he knows what it's like to come "home" to a hotel room instead of to his wife and children. His family misses him, too, and often he finds a little note or card in his luggage from his wife or one of his kids.

A couple of years ago, Bill was away on a trip and came across a note that his son, Alex, had smuggled into his luggage. Bill smiled as he read the crooked writing: "Alex loves Dad." What a great reminder of his loved ones at home! But then Bill noticed something else written on the paper. Turning it upside down, he read, "Dad loves Alex." His heart leaped! Bill was happy to read that Alex loved him, but to read that Alex *knew* his dad loved him...that was priceless![1]

God created us to give and receive love, not just with each other but with Him as well. He's our loving Father, and in many ways He constantly tells us, *"You are My child. I was delighted when you were born, and I love you still."* God loves hearing that we love Him, but how His heart must jump when He knows that we really *get it*, that we understand, receive, and delight in His love.

When we understand the Father-love of God, we naturally desire to spend time talking with Him. Prayer is no longer a duty; it becomes a delight! We recognize God not as an unapproachable entity, but as the loving Father who invites us to come straight to Him and tell Him what our day was like, what we'll face tomorrow, and how we feel about life.

Some of us have earthly fathers who loved us well; others of us have been deeply hurt by our fathers. Either way, God wants us to experience the fullness of a heavenly Father in His steady, consistent love. As Bill says, "On God's daisy there is no 'He loves me not.'"

DISCUSSION OPENERS

1. Complete this sentence: "I know God loves me because…" Let's create a list of all the ways God shows His love.

2. Think back over the last month. Tell of a time when you really experienced your Father's love. If you have a hard time remembering, ask God to show you glimpses of Himself acting as your heavenly Father.

3. Parents, share with your children the kinds of things you like to hear them tell you. Then, as a family, tell those kinds of things to your heavenly Father.

SCRIPTURES FOR GOING DEEPER

Luke 15:11–31

John 15:9–12

A PRAYER

Father, we love You. Thank You for loving us.
We like these times of talking with You and listening to You.
When we get busy with our day, please remind us of Your presence.
When we want to pull away from You, please remind us
that You never pull away from us.
When we shy away from Your discipline,
please remind us that it's part of Your love.
Thank You, Father, that Your love is steady and constant
and that You always want to hear from Your children.
In Jesus' name, amen.

A PARTING THOUGHT

"Love God and you will always be speaking to Him."

JEAN-NICHOLAS GROU[2]

A Loving Father

Approaching God as a Father may be easy if you've had a good earthly father. But if your dad was less than what God intended (and to some extent every father is), seeing God as a good and loving Father might be more difficult for you. If you or someone in your family has experienced the absence of a good and loving father, spend some time with the Scriptures for Going Deeper in this devotion. As a family, discuss the characteristics of a good father and how God exhibits those characteristics. Then pray that each of you can know and feel the Father's love. If necessary, ask God to show you how to talk with and/or forgive your earthly father.

Faith That Moves a Mountain

And Jesus answered and said to them,
"Truly I say to you, if you have faith and do not doubt,
you will not only do what was done to the fig tree, but even if you say to
this mountain, 'Be taken up and cast into the sea,' it shall happen."
MATTHEW 21:21 (NASB)

After World War II, many half-Japanese/half-American and half-Japanese/half-European children were abandoned in Japan, left to die by a society that placed no value on their little lives. But Christian missionaries, seeing the children's plight, started orphanages. In one of these orphanages Irene Smith, an English missionary, cared for twenty-two of these outcast children.

One night one of Irene's orphans, who was sick and bedridden, heard a sermon about how having small faith can enable a person to accomplish great things. In the supporting Scripture, Jesus told His disciples that if they had faith and didn't doubt, they could not only perform "small" feats such as making a fig tree wither as He had, but they could overcome much bigger obstacles with their prayers such as moving mountains and casting them into the sea.

This story caught the little invalid's attention for good reason. This little girl wished to see the Japanese Inland Sea again. She couldn't go to the beach herself because of her illness, and a huge mountain sat in front of the old building that housed the orphanage, blocking her view of her beloved sea.

At bedtime that night, the little girl asked to pray that God would move that mountain. Irene kindly replied, "No, God doesn't want to move a big mountain like that. After all, if He put that mountain there, why would He want to move it? When Jesus made that statement, He meant we should pray about the big mountains of trials in our lives."

"But, Miss Irene, it says if you have faith and do not doubt, the mountain will move. God is great, and He could do this. The Bible says so."

"Then go ahead and pray, child," Irene responded.

So every night the other orphan girls joined the sick child at her bedside and agreed together according to Matthew 18:19–20, earnestly praying that God would move the mountain so the sick little girl could see the sea.

Irene temporarily left the orphanage while on furlough to England. Months later, upon her return, she walked into the dormitory and found all the little girls clustered in front of the window. Looking out, Irene could hardly believe what she saw: the Japanese Inland Sea!

"What happened to the mountain?" Irene exclaimed, amazed.

"All we know is that we saw many kinds of bulldozers going up and down the mountain moving dirt," the girls answered, their eyes lit up with joy.

Curious about this mystery, Irene went to the town office and spoke with the local authorities about the mountain's disappearance. The mayor explained that coastal waves were eroding the land, so they needed the earth from the mountain to backfill the coastline.

Sure enough, they moved the mountain and "cast it into the sea."

A few months later, the little girl who had prayed to move mountains died. And eventually, the old building housing the orphanage was torn down. But the view of the Japanese Inland Sea is still there, many years later, and Irene learned a valuable lesson about faith.[1]

DISCUSSION OPENERS

1. Do you hesitate to take any Bible passages literally? Why or why not?

2. How does faith affect how you pray?

3. Is there a "mountain" or obstacle in your life you would like to see God move? If so, what kind of encouragement can you find from the God who parted the Red Sea, brought down the walls of Jericho, shut the mouths of lions, and did many other amazing things? Remember these miracles as you pray about the mountains in your own life.

SCRIPTURES FOR GOING DEEPER

Genesis 18:1–14
Numbers 23:19
James 1:6

A PRAYER

Lord, grant us the faith we need to believe all Your promises
and to pray, trusting You to intervene and move
even those things that look impossible or immovable.
As we wait for You to answer all our petitions,
let us hope in Your faithfulness and confidently rest in You.
In Jesus' name, amen.

A PARTING THOUGHT

"Faith comes from looking at God, not at the mountain."

BILL HYBELS

THREE

Tad Lincoln and His Dad

Let us then approach the throne of grace with confidence, so that we may receive mercy and find grace to help us in our time of need.

HEBREWS 4:16

When Abraham Lincoln was president of the United States, the White House was an imposing place. The nation was headed toward civil war and tensions were running high. It wasn't a time for fun and play.

But someone forgot to tell that to Tad and Willie (or, as history books remember them, Theodore and William) Lincoln. The magnificent White House was their home and personal playground. Tad especially was a young man of high spirits, and during the Civil War he wanted to do all he could to help out. So he decided to raise money to help wounded soldiers. Tad's fund-raising ideas included holding lawn sales of Abe's and Mary's clothes, providing goat cart rides through the White House corridors, and selling concessions to people waiting to see the president.

One day, Tad realized that his access to his famous father might also have monetary value. So Tad poked his head around the door to the Oval Office and asked Abraham Lincoln to meet some of his friends. Of course, Abe agreed. Tad invited one friend in, asked him his name, then introduced him to the president. This confused Abe a bit. Sure, the family hadn't lived in Washington, D.C., very long, but surely Tad would remember the names of his friends, wouldn't he? A chat with his enterprising son uncovered the truth: Tad had simply found people willing to pay a nickel to meet Abe Lincoln. After all, it was for a good cause!

Tad had connections and wasn't afraid to use them to benefit others. To him, the famous Abraham Lincoln wasn't a great president; he was just Dad.

We, too, have an incredible Father, one we might find intimidating to approach. But God freely invites His children to call Him "Abba" (the Aramaic word for "Daddy") and lets us poke our heads around the door to His throne room anytime we want. We can bring others to meet Him (for free!) or just enter by ourselves for a prayer chat.

Sometimes we might feel disconnected from God and find it difficult to pray. But God wants us to come to Him anyway. Even when we aren't at our best (especially at such times), He invites us to climb into His lap and tell Him all about our struggles. The more we seek Him in His throne room, the more any distance we feel from Him will melt away. And the closer we grow to Him, the more we'll want to continue seeking Him in prayer.

DISCUSSION OPENERS

1. How is your relationship with your heavenly Father? (Young children may enjoy drawing their answers to this question.)

2. Pray for each other based on each person's answer to the previous question. Remember, each of you has an individual relationship with God; members of the same family may be in different places in their walks with Him. If someone feels close to God, thank and praise Him for that. If, however, someone feels distant or is struggling in his or her relationship with God, ask how you can pray for that person.

SCRIPTURES FOR GOING DEEPER

Romans 8:15–16
1 John 4:18–19

A PRAYER

"Abba."
What a privilege to call You "Daddy!"
and come to You anytime and with everything that happens in our lives.
We can picture ourselves now coming into Your throne room and climbing
up on Your lap to tell You about our day.
Thank You for loving us and listening to all the little, silly things we say.
It's good to have a Daddy. We like being Your children!
In Jesus' name, amen.

A PARTING THOUGHT

"Heaven will be filled with five-year-olds."

BRENNAN MANNING

FOUR

Mr. Lump

*Casting the whole of your care—all your anxieties, all your worries, all
your concerns, once and for all—on Him; for He cares for you
affectionately and cares about you watchfully.*

1 PETER 5:7 (AMP)

Kristi and her seven-year-old son Michael perched on
kitchen stools and discussed worry. Only a few days
before, while Michael's dad, Jeff, gave Michael a bedtime hug, Jeff felt a lump on Michael's arm bone near his shoulder.

Now for most families, a lump isn't a worrisome thing, just the
result of falling on the playground or being hit with a baseball during
a neighborhood game. But for Michael and his parents, a lump caused
great concern. You see, at the young age of seven, Michael was a cancer survivor.

When he was less than one year old, Michael had endured aggressive chemotherapy, radiation, and a bone marrow transplant to treat a
rapidly advancing case of leukemia. His family faced the uncertainty of
Michael's health and the burden of a $205,000 bill for the bone mar-
row transplant, a procedure their insurance didn't cover. But they had
seen God's faithfulness over and over. Not only did Michael go into
remission, but God also provided for his care through a whole community that rallied to raise the money for the transplant.

Now, with Michael in remission for more than five years, his family faced a new challenge. An X ray showed a mass on the bone, and in a few days Michael would undergo further tests at the children's hospital in Portland, Oregon.

"What are the doctors going to do?" he asked his mom.

"They're going to look at Mr. Lump and do some more tests." Mr. Lump was the family's affectionate name for the bump on Michael's bone.

"Will it hurt?" The first time Michael had leukemia he was too young to know what was happening. This time, he was old enough to be a little worried. So when Kristi picked up the Bible for their time with God before homeschooling that day, she found herself turning to 1 Peter 5:6–7 (NASB). "Let's look and see what God's Word says," Kristi told Michael.

"Humble yourselves, therefore, under the mighty hand of God, that He may exalt you at the proper time, casting all your anxiety upon Him, because He cares for you," she read. Kristi then explained that "anxiety" meant a worry or a problem. "Whatever bothers you, any problem or worry, Jesus wants to take it because He loves you even more than Mommy and Daddy do, and we love you so much!"

Then Kristi asked her son a familiar question: "What does this verse mean to *you*, honey?"

"It means that I can put Mr. Lump in Jesus' hand, and I don't have to worry!" Michael replied, his blue eyes sparkling with confidence.

His mom's heart leaped. This seven-year-old understood for himself Peter's exhortation. Most importantly, he trusted God. After that day, Michael truly didn't worry.

At bedtime prayers each night with his family, Michael asked Jesus to take Mr. Lump away if that was His will. But Michael possessed an amazing, simple trust that enabled him to *leave his lump with Jesus*, whereas most of us are tempted to pick up our "lumps," take them back, carry them ourselves, or try to help God fix them.

A week later, Michael underwent a series of tests: a CAT scan, a bone scan, an ultrasound, and later an MRI. From that evidence, the doctors told the family they believed the lump was a benign mass produced from previous chemotherapy and radiation, and nothing to worry about. But Michael already knew not to worry. He'd given his lump to Jesus.[1]

DISCUSSION OPENERS

1. What is your "Mr. Lump"? Whatever your lump is, you can give it to Jesus because He loves and cares for you so much!

2. What happened when Michael let Jesus carry his burden? How did he feel? Why do you suppose he felt this way?

3. Michael's parents have tried to communicate to him their belief that prayer isn't a formula for getting certain results but rather an invitation to enjoy a wonderful and close relationship with their heavenly Father. Their faith in God was forged in the fires of tremendous difficulties and trials when Michael battled leukemia. How can prayer about your "Mr. Lump" draw you even closer to God?

SCRIPTURES FOR GOING DEEPER

Psalm 103:2–5
Isaiah 41:10
Jeremiah 17:14
John 14:1

A PRAYER

Jesus, we cast our burdens and cares on You because You've asked us to.
Thank You for the invitation!
Thank You that You cared for us so much that You carried our sins,
our burdens, and all our sicknesses and "lumps" on Yourself
while on the cross.
Help us to depend on You with a childlike trust
and to love You more each day.
In Jesus' name, amen.

A PARTING THOUGHT

"We need to learn to know Him so well that we feel safe when we have left our difficulties with Him. To know Jesus in that way is a prerequisite of all true prayer."

O. HALLESBY

FIVE

When We Ask for a Fish

You do not have because you do not ask.

JAMES 4:2B (NASB)

When Dick's son, Aaron, was eight years old, Dick purchased a rod, reel, and fishing tackle for him. That summer father and son fished together occasionally, and Aaron actually caught a few small ones.

When August rolled around, Dick had a two-week speaking engagement at a campground in northern Ohio. He took his family with him, including Aaron and all the fishing gear. On the first day the sun was bright, the water a vivid blue, and the fish were jumping—or so they'd heard. Aaron broke out the tackle and went fishing in the camp lake. He sat patiently for over an hour. Nothing. But he was not deterred. Fishing the camp lake became a new challenge. Each day, Aaron spent two or three hours fishing from that lonely shore…and each day he came back to their cabin empty-handed.

Dick took his son to local fishing experts who advised them concerning bait and hot spots on the lake, and Aaron tried their suggestions. But he always returned from his fishing vigils sad and defeated, toting an empty stringer.

On the last day of camp, Dick decided to step in and help. He borrowed a rowboat and loaded their gear. At the last minute, Sarah,

Aaron's older sister, joined them. They pushed off from shore and headed for the hot spot the local experts had recommended.

They rowed out, baited and dropped their lines, and waited. It wasn't long before Sarah caught a large, ugly carp. As she hauled the heavy fish into the boat, tears began to stream down Aaron's face. He had faithfully fished for two weeks, only to have his sister catch the big one on her first try.

Dick assured Aaron that there were other fish in the lake and that he could use all three fishing lines. Again they waited. And waited. Time passed slowly: fifteen minutes, thirty, finally an hour. Nothing. In frustration, Dick looked up to the sky and shouted, "Lord? Why can't you help this boy catch a fish?"

At that precise moment, Aaron caught a fish larger than his sister's.

Not wanting to tempt God, they rowed to shore. As Dick held the boat and his kids climbed out, Aaron beamed from ear to ear. "Dad," he said, "this must be your lucky day for answered prayer!"

DISCUSSION OPENERS

1. What happened when Aaron's dad called out to God for help? How can this story encourage you to ask God for something you need?

2. Do you ever think God tires of us asking Him for things? Read the Scriptures for Going Deeper, then discuss this question again.

3. The Bible describes earthly moms and dads as "evil" (that is, compared to the righteousness of God), yet when our babies cry for food or our children ask for something, we delight to give them what they need or want. How do you feel toward your heavenly Father when He supplies something you've asked for? How do you think God feels?

SCRIPTURES FOR GOING DEEPER

Matthew 7:7
Matthew 7:11
James 1:5

A PRAYER

Lord, forgive us for the times we don't ask
but instead barrel through situations trying to provide for ourselves
when You stand willing and able to provide good things
for those who ask.
Thank You that You never tire of us coming to Your throne of grace
for mercy and help in time of need!
In Jesus' name, amen.

A PARTING THOUGHT

"God will not disappoint us by not answering; neither will He deny us by giving us some other thing for which we have not asked...or by opening to us the wrong door at which we were not knocking. If we ask for bread, He will give us bread. If we ask for an egg, He will give us an egg. If we ask for a fish, He will give us a fish. Not something like bread, but bread itself will be given unto us. Not something like a fish, but a fish will be given. Not evil will be given to us in answer to prayer, but good!"

E. M. BOUNDS

SIX

Hotline to Heaven

*Call to Me and I will answer you, and I will tell you
great and mighty things, which you do not know.*
JEREMIAH 33:3 (NASB)

Sandy, a preschool teacher, had been asking God to show her
how she could teach her students to pray. One day He gave
her a creative idea: the "Jesus Phone." That day a play telephone located in one of the play centers' kitchens became the kids' hotline to heaven.

Sandy introduced the idea to the preschoolers as they sat in a circle
discussing their lesson for the morning. In the middle of the discussion
she suddenly put her finger over her mouth and said quietly, *"Shhhhh,*
children—I hear something." She listened with her ear cocked toward
the "source" of the noise, then said, "No, I guess not. Let's go on."

In a few minutes she interrupted the story she was telling and said,
"Oh, I'm sure I heard a phone. I think it's over here in the kitchen,…and
it's definitely ringing. Let's go see who it is."

As the kids ran to the kitchen, Phyllis, the other teacher, picked up
the phone and put the receiver to her ear. "Wouldn't you know, *Jesus* is
on the phone!" Phyllis said. "What would you like to tell Him?"

The children spilled out all the things they wanted to say to Jesus:
"I got hurt at school."

"My puppy bit me."

"No one will play with me at school, Jesus."

Later that afternoon, one of the boys, Drew, got in trouble for kicking another child. Tired and hot from teaching kids all day, Phyllis's first instinct was to scold the little troublemaker. Then she remembered the Jesus Phone.

"Drew, do you hear something? I think it's the Jesus Phone. Yes, it is!" She picked up the receiver.

"Hello, Jesus. What's that? Oh, you see that Drew is having a hard day. Oh yes, Lord, You want to tell him You love him and forgive him and want to help him have a better day. Okay, I'll tell him.... What's that?...You want to know if he'll apologize to Kyler?"

She put her hand over the mouthpiece and asked Drew if he'd apologize. He nodded yes and went to ask his classmate's forgiveness. Kyler forgave Drew, the two kids hugged, and the teacher said goodbye to Jesus.

Just as Phyllis was about to hang up, a four-year-old girl ran over and jumped in her lap. "Don't hang up!" she exclaimed. "I need to talk to Jesus, too!"

Through this simple, concrete device these young children grasped the truth that they could talk to Jesus and He'd really listen. They learned that they could be themselves and talk about their heart's desires and disappointments just as they'd talk with a friend.

You have a direct line to heaven, too.

These days, when we call banks or schools or businesses—even churches, for that matter—we usually reach voice mail or an answering machine. We can so easily think God treats our "calls" to Him in the same way:

If you're sick, press 9.

If you're concerned about a friend, press 2.

If you're interested in global evangelism and want a missionary sent to a certain nation, press 6.

If you need a personal visit from one of our angels, press A.

To confess a sin, press C.

To leave a message for God, wait for the harp.

Can you imagine calling someone at any time of day or night and not having to hear an impersonal answering machine message? Can you imagine never hearing a busy signal, never listening to static-filled music while on hold, never being interrupted by call waiting?

Guess what? The God of the universe is waiting for your call! You have a direct line to the Creator of every big thing who wants you to tell Him about even the small things that bother you. And that's what prayer is: your very own hotline to heaven. No "wait for the beep" or "excuse me while I check this other call." The King of kings is always there, He always listens, and He invites you to His throne of grace for all the help you need.

Author and speaker Corrie ten Boom called Jeremiah 33:3 "God's private telephone number." He's given it to you—call it often!

DISCUSSION OPENERS

1. Why do you think the "Jesus Phone" helped the children talk to God more easily?

2. How do you feel when someone puts you on hold or you reach voice mail instead of talking to a real person? Describe what goes through your mind when you're talking with someone and he or she says, "Oh, excuse me, I have another call coming in on call waiting."

3. How can we know that God hears us whenever we pray? Read the Scriptures for Going Deeper to find out, then thank God for the wonderful opportunity He has given us to reach Him directly.

4. Have you ever talked with a friend who did *all* the talking, not letting you get a word in edgewise? How did that make you feel? Have you ever prayed and prayed about something, then realized *you* were doing all the talking? How do you suppose God felt about that? Once we feel comfortable talking to God, we often forget to listen—thus missing out on His words for us about our problem or issue. Be sure to save time to listen quietly to God after you've presented your needs to Him so He can answer you!

SCRIPTURES FOR GOING DEEPER

Psalm 62:5–8

Psalm 145:18

Philippians 4:6–7

A PRAYER

Lord, what a wonder,
what an amazing thing prayer is,
that You want to talk to us
and You want to listen to everything we want to say!
Help us talk to You just as easily
as those children spoke to You on their Jesus Phone
and just as naturally as a child pours out her heart to her mother.
In Jesus' name, amen.

A PARTING THOUGHT

"Be yourself. Be natural before God. Do not pretend to emotions you do not feel. Tell him whatever is on your heart and mind with whatever words are most natural to you. You do not have to speak to him in 'religious' language about 'spiritual' matters only.... Speak as naturally and as easily as you would to a friend, since God is just that."

GEORGE MACDONALD

SEVEN

A House of Prayer

My house shall be called a house of prayer.
MATTHEW 21:13 (NASB)

The Lord is not slow about His promise, as some count slowness,
but is patient toward you, not wishing for any to perish
but for all to come to repentance.
2 PETER 3:9 (NASB)

When a Washington family began praying regularly for their neighbors, exciting things started happening.

Lewie Schultz, the dad, proposed that each member of his family choose five people in their neighborhood and pray five blessings for those people five minutes a day for five weeks. Lewie's family agreed, so each member of the family, even the three-year-old, chose five neighbors to pray for. At bedtime prayers, family devotions, and morning breakfast, the Schultzes lifted their neighbors to the throne of grace and blessed them.

As they prayed, God started working. Sarah, the seven-year-old, prayed for two friends down the street. One day the mother of those two girls stopped Sarah's mom at the grocery store and asked if she and her daughters could attend church with the Schultz family. The next Sunday this mom committed her life to Christ and began praying earnestly for her husband. While her husband was away on an extended business trip, he woke up one morning in a hotel praying to the Lord. Previously indifferent to the gospel, he began to attend church and a few weeks later accepted Christ. Soon the whole family was baptized!

God also touched the family on the corner. The Schultzes prayed the five blessings on that household, specifically asking God to bless the dad's labor and give him favor at his job as a policeman. Before long, this policeman's wife told Lewie that he'd received a promotion to detective. Lewie went home and shared the good news with his kids: "We've prayed for our neighbor to have God's favor at work, so we can thank God for that promotion." And they all rejoiced together.

As the Schultzes continue to pray, God builds bridges between them and their neighbors. The aspiring rock musician next door, a teenager who had terrorized the neighborhood, became receptive to Lewie sharing new CDs of Christian rock groups, and they've begun to build a relationship. Two moms asked if their kids could go to AWANA (a Christian club) at the Schultzes' church, and the moms themselves attended a women's outreach dinner. Lewie's five-year-old, Peter, had prayed for a little boy in their community, and God gave Peter an opportunity to talk with that little boy about Christ one day on the playground.

This family doesn't feel they've "arrived." Like the rest of us, they struggle with consistency in praying for their neighbors. But the children have seen their friends impacted by their prayers and the neighborhood families touched by God. They've seen small miracles and big ones.

But the Schultzes are only one family praying, and they have a bigger vision: that prayer partners would eventually "adopt" every one of the 275 homes in their development, literally saturating the area in prayer.

Who's praying for your neighborhood?

DISCUSSION OPENERS

1. Since our homes belong to the Lord, what if each of our families becomes a "house of prayer" for our neighborhoods or circles of friends? Brainstorm together what God could do with a prayed-for

community where every person is covered in blessings. What might He want to do where you live, work, and play as *you* pray?

2. When Lewie heard how his unsaved neighbor woke up praying during a business trip, God's Spirit spoke to him and said, "See, when you began praying, I started working." How does the Spirit want to work in your neighbors' lives? Write down their names and begin to pray for them regularly.

3. Since God said in His Word that He doesn't want any people to perish but all to turn to Him and enjoy life in heaven, how could that direct your petitions for those around you who don't know God yet?

SCRIPTURES FOR GOING DEEPER

Matthew 9:38

Acts 9:1–19

Acts 12:5–12

A PRAYER

Lord, give us a heart and burden for our neighbors
to know and love You.
Give us the kind of compassion and caring Jesus had
and show us what You're calling us to do as a family.
Make our home a house of prayer!
Right now we want to bring our neighbors, _____,
to Your throne of grace.
In Jesus' name, amen.

A PARTING THOUGHT

"What might God do in a prayed-for world? It's likely that God has never had such a thing before, in which every breathing person had been prayed for by caring Christians. Step into this movement of holy expectancy. God will not bring revival by surprise. Scripture hints that God will be pleased to visit a prayed-for world."

STEVE HAWTHORNE

The Five Blessings

Each member of the Schultz family prayed five blessings for five neighbors five minutes a day for five weeks, a prayer plan suggested in the H.O.P. E. (Houses of Prayer Everywhere) 5x5x5 Plan. In this prayer plan, each area of blessing begins with a letter from the word "bless":

B (Body)—Blessings on a neighbor's physical body, including health, strength, protection, and safety.

L (Labor)—Blessings on a neighbor's work, income, and security, or, if a child, on his or her studies.

E (Emotional)—Blessings on a neighbor's emotional well-being, especially that he or she can trust God, be free from worry and fear, and experience joy, peace, and hope.

S (Social)—Blessings on relationships, such as those between husband and wife, parents and kids.

S (Spiritual)—Blessings on a neighbor for salvation, faith, and grace.

If you'd like more information on the H.O.P. E. 5x5x5 Plan, call 1-800-217-5200 to order the *Make Your Home a Power House* booklet, the *Five Blessings Brochure,* or the *Personal Lighthouse Kit,* which includes a video.

EIGHT

God's Power and a Gray-Striped Cat

~~~

Jesus called a small child over to him and
set the little fellow down among them, and said,
"Unless you turn to God from your sins and become as little children,
you will never get into the Kingdom of Heaven.
Therefore anyone who humbles himself as this little child is
the greatest in the Kingdom of Heaven."

MATTHEW 18:2–4 (TLB)

One day many summers ago, a gray-striped cat showed up at the Wittmans' back door. Maureen Wittman placed a classified ad in the lost and found section of the local newspaper and posted signs throughout the neighborhood. When her husband, Robert, took his evening walk with their four children, the cat tagged along. And although Robert asked all the neighbors if they knew the cat or her owner, no one claimed her.

Quickly, the situation became annoying. Katy, the Wittmans' house cat, disapproved of the intruder and let the family know it. So late one evening Robert put the gray-striped cat in his car, drove a couple of miles to a park, and left her there.

But the next morning when the family arose, there sat a gray-striped cat staring at them through the window. Maureen knew then and there that this cat had adopted them for good. The family appropriately named the new cat "Squatter," a term the dictionary defines as "one who settles on land without rights or permission." The Wittmans fed her and took her to the veterinarian for a checkup, shots, and spaying. But it was too late for that last procedure; Squatter was already pregnant.

In due time, Squatter delivered six fluffy kittens who instantly won the hearts of the Wittman children. As the kittens grew, Squatter took them on walks and showed them how to hunt chipmunks. Maureen made "Free Kittens" signs to post in the yard, but she never got to use them because one morning Squatter took her kittens on their daily stroll and never returned. This broke the children's hearts. The Wittmans asked neighbors, made signs, and petitioned God to help them find Squatter and her kittens. But after several days of searching the neighborhood to no avail, Maureen and her husband concluded that Animal Control must have picked up the cats and put them to sleep.

For the next two years, Maureen's children prayed every night for Squatter and the kittens. Every night they asked God to protect and help them. Maureen didn't have the heart to tell her kids the cats were long gone. As time went on and they kept praying for Squatter and her clan, Maureen thought more than once, *Oh, God, You're so patient with the kids' constant asking. They just don't know the cats have been destroyed. Should I tell them?*

Then one day a neighbor asked Maureen if she had ever met the man who lived four doors down the street from her. When Maureen said she hadn't, the neighbor explained that a gray-striped cat and six kittens had appeared at this man's back door almost two years before. The cat came to visit every day until the man finally took her in—along with her brood. He gave the gray-striped cat to his sister, kept one of the kittens as his own, and found good homes for the rest.

As the neighbor relayed the story, Maureen could hear the Lord say, "Oh ye of little faith! Your children never gave up hope, and I have answered their prayer." When Maureen told her kids, they weren't flabbergasted as she had been. They knew all along that God was watching over Squatter and her kittens; after all, they had asked Him to, hadn't they?

Through her children, this mom learned a lesson about persevering prayer and childlike faith that she never forgot.

DISCUSSION OPENERS

1. Maureen once teasingly asked her children if Jesus' exhortation to "become like little children" meant that she should spill her milk and run around and dance when she should be sleeping. They giggled and answered, "Nooooo, Mommy, it means that you should love Him without thinking about it!" What do *you* think Jesus' exhortation means?

2. The kids in this story prayed with perseverance because they loved the kittens, and God rewarded their steadfastness. In the two years when the kids knew nothing about the cats, how was God answering their prayers about protecting and caring for Squatter and her kittens?

3. Have you been praying about something for a long time, wishing God would answer? Don't give up! Keep praying until something happens. God may just blow your mind with His answer at just the right time.

SCRIPTURES FOR GOING DEEPER

Matthew 7:7–8

(Note that when these verses say "ask," "seek," and "knock," they really mean "ask and keep on asking," "seek and keep on seeking," "knock and keep on knocking.")

Galatians 6:9

Ephesians 6:18

A PRAYER

Lord, for the problems and needs that concern us,
no matter how small or big,
give us the grace to approach You boldly and confidently
with the faith these children had in Your power.
Strengthen us so we'll persevere and won't give up asking;
direct our prayers into agreement with Your plan,
and give us thankful hearts whatever the outcome.
In Jesus' name, amen.

A PARTING THOUGHT

"By perseverance the snail reached the ark."

CHARLES SPURGEON

NINE

The Way That I Take

But he knows the way that I take; when he has tested me,
I will come forth as gold.

JOB 23:10

he hot noon sun blazed as the horses plodded along the dusty China road. The wagon was especially heavy that day since Peter Kiehn was bringing more than three hundred pounds of silver and copper coins to his fellow missionaries at Yucheng.

As he passed through village after village thronged with people, he thought back to that morning. He and other missionaries had gathered in the mission office to pray before setting out their separate ways. As Peter left the office, he noticed two plaques hanging above the door. The top one read, HE KNOWETH THE WAY THAT I TAKE. That phrase engraved itself in his mind. Now, lulled by the thwop of the horses' hooves in front of him and the ch-ching of the coins behind him, Peter's mind dwelled on the promise: *He knows the way that I take.*

The horses were hot and panting, so Peter stopped at the next village to buy water for them. Usually when he stopped in a village, hordes of people would throng around to see and touch the stranger, and Peter would take advantage of the opportunity to preach about Jesus. But this time the village people kept their distance, peeping cautiously around corners, through door cracks, and over the walls lining the streets. "Are the people restless for some reason?" he asked the old man selling water.

After glancing in all directions to make sure no one would overhear him, the man replied, "We have heard there are bandits on the road." This wasn't unusual in that part of China at that time. Farmers who were "respectable" citizens often led double lives as bandits who robbed neighbors and kidnapped anyone they could hold for ransom. Rich foreigners were especially easy marks.

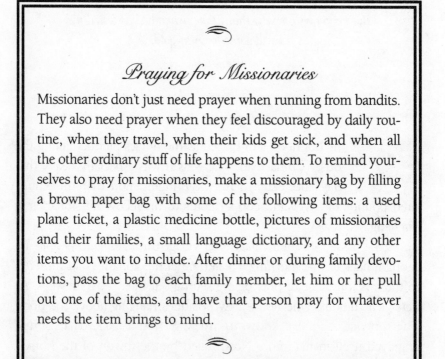

Praying for Missionaries

Missionaries don't just need prayer when running from bandits. They also need prayer when they feel discouraged by daily routine, when they travel, when their kids get sick, and when all the other ordinary stuff of life happens to them. To remind yourselves to pray for missionaries, make a missionary bag by filling a brown paper bag with some of the following items: a used plane ticket, a plastic medicine bottle, pictures of missionaries and their families, a small language dictionary, and any other items you want to include. After dinner or during family devotions, pass the bag to each family member, let him or her pull out one of the items, and have that person pray for whatever needs the item brings to mind.

That was all Peter needed to know. He jumped into his wagon and started away from the village. Thinking of the danger he faced, he remembered the words from that morning: *He knows the way that I take.*

Suddenly he heard heavy footsteps behind him. He spun around and saw men heading toward him, each waving a gun. Knowing he couldn't escape, Peter stopped the wagon. The bandits were excited to capture a foreigner with not only clothes, a watch, and horses—but all that money, too. What a haul!

The bandits huddled together and considered places to take Peter for hiding. As Peter listened, he realized that none of the villages the bandits mentioned were anywhere near. "O God, you know the way that I take," he breathed.

Finally the bandits settled on a destination. Forcing him back into the wagon, they set off with Peter driving at gunpoint. They stopped just outside a village and made Peter remove his outer clothes, his shoes, and his watch. They took his bedding and all the money from the wagon. Then the leader asked, mockingly, "Are you happy now?" Thinking back to the quiet morning of prayer in the office, Peter resolutely answered, "Yes. Jesus knows the way that I take."

"Then get on and hurry to that village," the leader said, "or we shoot."

Peter hurried. Inexplicably, the bandits had let him keep his wagon and horses. The village opened its gate to let him in...but they wouldn't let him stay for fear of reciprocity from the bandits. The gatekeepers ordered him to go through town and out the gate on the far side. Peter pleaded with them to let him stay within the city walls, but they wouldn't listen. The whole town faced danger if they harbored a foreigner. They led Peter through the town and opened the far gate. As the gate closed behind his wagon, Peter knew he had a long way to go before finding safety again.

He glanced behind and with dismay saw the bandits again! They were riding around the town wall, trying to enter the town by the gate that had just closed behind him. When the band saw the familiar wagon and horses, they urged their horses to pursue him. They had said they would shoot, now they meant it!

Peter had no choice but to use his whip on the horses, urging them to run faster, and to pray, pray, pray! The road turned uphill, and as Peter's horses tired of running, the bandits closed the gap. Peter was desperate. Could he make it up the hill in time? "O God, help me *now*, for you know the way I take!" he cried out loud.

Suddenly he saw another group of riders pouring over the top of the hill. His heart sank. Now he was caught between *two* groups of bandits!

But as his horses drew nearer, he saw he was wrong. The group ahead of him was government cavalry. He was safe!

About a month after returning home safely from his encounter with the bandits, Peter saw in his morning mail a letter from an American acquaintance. "I don't know you very well," the man wrote, "but your whole family has been on my mind. My wife and I really felt like God was leading us to pray for you—has anything unusual come along your path?"

God did know Peter's path and the bandits that were on it. And through the power of prayer, He answered Peter's need. What a reminder to pray when God prompts us to. We never know when God is using our prayers to "send in the cavalry" half a world away.

DISCUSSION OPENERS

1. What do you think might have happened to Peter if someone hadn't prayed for him?

2. Have you ever had someone on your mind in a really strong way? If so, what did you do?

3. How does God prompt us to pray for others?

4. Who do you feel God is prompting you to pray for right now?

5. How can we remind ourselves to pray for others, especially missionaries?

SCRIPTURES FOR GOING DEEPER

Psalm 20:1–2

Acts 12:1–19

A PRAYER

Lord, forgive us for the times when You've prompted us to pray for someone
and we've ignored Your quiet whispering.
When You do bring someone or something to our minds,
help us to be quiet and listen.
Thank You for the fun of participating in Your ministry, even when
we don't know the whole story. We look forward to hearing it
when we get to heaven!

Until then, we want to be Your faithful pray-ers.
In Jesus' name, amen.

A PARTING THOUGHT

"Prayer moves the arm that moves the world."

THE SECOND MOTTO PETER SAW ON THE MISSION OFFICE WALL

TEN

Prayer Chorus

Devote yourselves to prayer, being watchful and thankful.
COLOSSIANS 4:2

o you remember the opening scene of the Christmas movie classic *It's a Wonderful Life*? As the movie begins, we see a small, snowcapped sign that says Welcome to Bedford Falls. More snow drifts down, reflecting the glow of Christmas lights and piling up along the small-town streets. Then we see the Gower Drug Store, the little church on the corner, Martini's, the Bedford Falls garage, and the Bailey house. And as we see these places, we hear the people inside. One by one, they're praying...

"I owe everything to George Bailey. Help him, dear Father."

"Help my son George tonight."

"He never thinks about himself, God. That's why he's in trouble."

"George is a good guy. Give him a break, God."

"I love him, dear Lord. Watch over him tonight."

And finally a little girl pleads, "Please, God, something's the matter with Daddy. Please bring Daddy back!"

Although each person prays alone, we hear the voices joining together, becoming a loud babble rising from all over the town, beseeching God to aid a man named George Bailey. God hears those prayers and, knowing George is in trouble, sends an angel to help him.

Prayer Chorus

To help you and your children imagine how a prayer chorus might sound to God, watch the opening scene of It's a Wonderful Life *together.*

Now *It's a Wonderful Life* is just a made-up story, but imagine that you could hear all the prayers in the world just as God can. Maybe the babble of prayer in the movie is what it really sounds like when God hears people all over a town—or even the world—praying for the same thing. Each voice may start out alone, but by the time it reaches God, it's part of a huge chorus asking for the same thing.

So even if you think you're alone in prayer, pray anyway. You never know who's praying with you! And you never know what God has planned....

DISCUSSION OPENERS

1. Have you ever found out that you and a friend were praying for the same thing and didn't know it? If so, how did that make you feel? And how did God answer your prayers?

2. What has God encouraged you to pray for? Consider some of the following questions:

- If you could help any one person in your school, workplace, or church, who would it be?
- If God said to you, "I'll do one thing you ask for any group of people you choose," whom would you select? Why?
- Do you feel compassion for certain a type of person (for example, homeless people, children without a father or mother, or schoolchildren who struggle to fit in)?
- How will your answers to these questions prompt you to pray?

3. Do you ever feel lonely when praying? If so, ask God to multiply your prayers and to call more people to join you in your petitions.

SCRIPTURES FOR GOING DEEPER

Daniel 9:23; 10:2–14

A PRAYER

Father God, please encourage us to devote ourselves to prayer.
Help us discern Your will and to pray in agreement with it.
And when we feel lonely in prayer, thinking our voices are small and don't
count,
help us remember we are not alone.
Use all our prayers, rising from all over the world and joining together,
to fulfill Your purposes.
Thank You for letting our small voices be a part of Your big plans.
In Jesus' name, amen.

A PARTING THOUGHT

"Units of prayer combined, like drops of water, make an ocean which defies resistance."

E. M. BOUNDS[1]

Praying for Your Local Schools

Your family can be part of the prayer chorus (joining Moms In Touch pray-ers, Christian teachers who are interceding, and others) for salvation and wisdom for all schoolteachers, principals, and staff; for an outpouring of God's Spirit so truth will be taught in all areas of the curriculum; and for every student to know Christ and grow in Him. You can pray before school, in evening family devotional times, and even pray a "drive-by" prayer whenever you pass the school buildings.[2]

ELEVEN

Lord, Save Me!

*The righteous cry, and the Lord hears and
delivers them out of all their troubles.*
PSALM 34:17 (NASB)

The disciples were exhausted after the long day with Jesus among the crowds. Peter could feel his tired muscles straining as he pulled the oars of the boat. He wanted to keep replaying the wonder of the day in his mind—how Jesus had fed all those people, how the food had appeared out of nowhere—but he was just too tired. And even worse, the gusting wind pushed against every stroke he took.

The disciples had wanted to stay with Jesus and savor the day, but He had firmly commanded them to sail across the lake. He wanted to spend the night alone, praying to God.

Peter had passed many nights on the water as a fisherman; he knew times like this. When it was pitch black in the small hours of the morning, when he was bone tired and still had hours to go, the wild wind and water could really play tricks on him. He'd even think he saw things when nothing was there.

Steadily, Peter and the others strained at the oars, battling the wind. Suddenly, next to him, John grabbed his arm. "Peter!" he yelled. "I think I saw something white…over there!"

Peter peered into the darkness but couldn't see a thing. "John," he yelled back, "You should know better. You always think there is some-thing in the night and there never is. Just row."

After a couple more strokes, John stopped cold. With fear in his voice, he shouted, "Peter, I see it again! I'm telling you, there's some-thing there!"

Peter paused in his rowing, again studying the darkness where John was pointing. Nothing.

Then, through a dip in the waves, he saw it too. Something white in the distance, floating just on top of the water...moving toward them! Soon the other disciples noticed it. Matthew, Andrew, Judas—they all stopped rowing.

"It's a ghost!" James cried.

All of a sudden it seemed everyone was talking at once. "Where?" "Over there!" "What does it want with us?" "I wish Jesus were here!"

Peter sat aghast, his knuckles white as he clenched the oars.

The white form came nearer and nearer, even though the wind was churning the waves more than ever. Now the disciples could clearly see that it had a man's shape.

It looked like it would go right past the boat when suddenly it turned and came straight toward them! It seemed to have a face, and hair plastered down by the water's spray. And then it spoke: "Take courage! It is I! Don't be afraid!"

What? Jesus? Peter's mind raced. No, of course not. They had left Jesus praying on the shore. This apparition couldn't be Jesus. He stared harder. He could barely see the face through the darkness, but it *did* look a little like Jesus. And the voice...it could be His. Before Peter knew it, he was shouting a wild challenge. "Lord, if it's You, tell me to come to You on the water!"

"Come!" the form replied.

Now *that* sounded like Jesus. Swallowing hard, Peter released the oars, stepped over the side of the boat, and...stood on the water! He took another step...and didn't sink! Another step closer and he could see now—it *really was* Jesus! Thrilled, he kept going. He was walking on water! Jesus grinned at Peter as he took step after step toward Him. But just then a blast of wind picked up a wave and drenched Peter's face in icy water. Startled, he looked down and saw the waves under his feet. *What am I doing?* Peter thought as fear clutched his stomach.

Instantly, he sank into the water. Just as his head was about to go under he cried, "Lord, save me!"

Immediately, Jesus reached down and caught Peter, lifting him from the water. The Master's eyes were like those of a loving, patient father with a reticent child. "Oh, Peter, you of little faith. Why did you doubt?"

As Peter and Jesus climbed in the boat, the other disciples moved back in silence to make room for them. Peter collapsed onto the hard seat, gasping. In amazement, he realized that as soon as Jesus had stepped into the boat, the wind had stopped howling. The boat no longer tossed about; it just rocked gently on the tranquil water. The silence was almost louder than the storm had been.

The disciples were stunned, barely able to take it all in. "Truly," John said, "You are the Son of God."[1]

DISCUSSION OPENERS

1. Why do you think Peter began to sink?

2. What happened when Peter prayed, "Lord, save me!"

3. Have you ever prayed a prayer like that? If so, what happened?

4. How many words did Peter pray? Sometimes we think we have to pray long prayers to get God's attention, but that's not so. Short, honest, simple prayers hit God's heart just as Peter's three-word prayer touched Jesus' heart. God hears, knows our hearts, and acts on our behalf based on His power and ability, not on our strength. As a way of thanking God, sing together "Jesus Loves Me, This I Know."

SCRIPTURES FOR GOING DEEPER

Psalm 46:1
Matthew 14:22–33
Hebrews 11:6

A PRAYER

Jesus, we feel scared so often
and think we're battling the wind and the waves of our lives alone.
We wonder how many times You've been right there, willing to help,
and we haven't seen You or have felt too scared to recognize You.
Help us live in the truth that You are a safe, safe place for our hearts.
We want to be near You and cry to You whenever we're angry, hurting, or
scared.
We're glad You listen to us just as we are!
In Jesus' name, amen.

A PARTING THOUGHT

"Prayer imparts the power to walk and not faint."

OSWALD CHAMBERS

TWELVE

Praying for Our Enemies

I'm telling you to love your enemies.
Let them bring out the best in you, not the worst.
When someone gives you a hard time, respond with the energies of prayer,
for then you are working out of your true selves, your God-created selves.

MATTHEW 5:44–45 (THE MESSAGE)

The milling crowd was restless. You could feel the antici-
pation even though it was only eight o'clock in the morning. Finally the crowd stirred and the yelling began.
Threats. Obscenities. Screaming. All because *they* were coming silently
down the street: the federal marshals…and the small, six-year-old girl
they were guarding. And when she walked home from school, frenzied
people again lined the streets screaming, cursing, and threatening to
kill her.

Why? Because Ruby Bridges was black, the first black child to attend
that all-white school. And in New Orleans in 1960, enough people
hated the idea of black and white children sitting in the same classroom
that Ruby needed protection from the daily barrage of hate.

You'd think that Ruby and her family would bow under the pressure. Even if she didn't quit school, surely she would become depressed
and frightened. But she didn't. Ruby was cheerful, happy to be in
school. Even her teacher couldn't understand it. "You know, I don't
understand this child," the teacher told Robert Coles, a psychiatrist

who was watching Ruby to see how she handled the pressure. "She seems so happy. She comes here so cheerfully."

Dr. Coles didn't understand it either. Surely, there was something wrong with Ruby that she just wasn't showing. She couldn't possibly be as cheerful as she appeared.

One day Ruby's teacher saw her stop outside the school and talk to the crowd. Startled, the teacher mentioned it to Dr. Coles.

That night, Dr. Coles went to Ruby's home to find out what had happened. "Ruby," he said, "your teacher told me she saw you talking to those people outside the school today."

"Oh, I wasn't talking to them," Ruby answered, "I was just saying a prayer for them."

Every day, Ruby and her family prayed for those screaming people. Why? "Because," Ruby explained, "they need praying for."[1]

Most of us don't face enemies everyday such as Ruby's. But we always have people in our lives who, for some reason, we consider our foes. When we come across such people, what should we do? Run? Get even? *No, God says. Love them. Love your enemies with the love that overflows from Me.*

A good, practical way to show love for your enemies is to pray for them. Have you ever noticed that it's really hard to ask God to help someone and still hold a grudge against that person? Praying for that person melts the bitterness, resentment, and dislike that we may otherwise feel.

Just ask Ruby.

DISCUSSION OPENERS

1. How do you think God felt watching the hate people poured on Ruby Bridges? (Remember that God is both just and merciful.)

2. *The Message* paraphrases Matthew 5:44 as "when someone gives you a hard time, respond with the energies of prayer." When someone hurts you, what do you devote your energies to: getting angry, getting even, pouting, telling all your friends, holding a grudge? How does God want you to use your energies? What good things can happen when you pray for someone who hurts you?

3. Who is your "enemy" right now? Are you willing to pray for him or her? What do you think that person really needs? What do you think God wants for him or her?

SCRIPTURES FOR GOING DEEPER

Matthew 6:12
Romans 5:6–11; 12:17–21

A PRAYER

Father, we're thinking about our "enemies" and what they've done to us.
Our hurt is real, God.
Please let us feel Your comforting touch on our hearts.
But also help us remember that when we were still Your enemies,
You loved us and gave Your Son Jesus so we could live.
Help us begin to love the people who have hurt us
with just a bit of the love You have for us.
Fill our hearts with Your forgiveness.
In Jesus' name, amen.

A PARTING THOUGHT

"It took me a long time to understand that God is not the enemy of my enemies. God is not even the enemy of God's enemies."

PASTOR MARTIN NIEMOLLER, WHO WAS IMPRISONED BY THE NAZIS[2]

THIRTEEN

A Christmas Prayer

Every desirable and beneficial gift comes out of heaven.
The gifts are rivers of light cascading down from the Father of Light.
JAMES 1:17 (THE MESSAGE)

ark's family had recently arrived in the African country of Angola and were facing their first Christmas away from family and friends. They already knew it would be difficult, but then they heard that their Christmas packages sent from back home wouldn't arrive until January or February. With the sparse toy selection in Luanda, the city where they lived, their four-year-old daughter, Breanna, wouldn't find many presents under the Christmas tree.

So one December day, Mark explained the situation to Breanna, then asked her what she wanted for Christmas. She quickly responded, "A kitty cat!"

Though Mark didn't particularly like cats, he couldn't find any other gifts for his daughter, so he went cat hunting. But while plenty of dogs live in Angola, Mark soon discovered that cats were scarce. He searched all over the city, and the only cats he found lived on the United Nations compound.

So with Breanna in tow, Mark looked in gardens and behind brick walls and under porches. He searched behind trash cans and asked every person they met for tips on finding stray cats. Even after looking in every likely place a kitty might hide, they couldn't find any kittens. And the larger cats on the compound eluded every attempt at capture.

Finally, Mark knelt down, gently took his daughter's hand, and said, "I'm sorry, honey. There just aren't any kittens here for you. Let's go home."

"But Daddy, where are we going to get a kitten?" Breanna asked, with a sad face that almost broke her father's heart.

Having no idea, he responded, "I guess you'll just have to pray and ask Jesus to bring you a kitty for Christmas."

Right on the street they bowed their heads, and Breanna earnestly asked the Lord to bring her a kitty for Christmas.

As the December days flew by, they still had found no kitten. Just a few days before Christmas Mark went to his neighbor's garage to charge the battery in his neighbor's car. (This neighbor had gone to the U.S. in June, leaving his house and car in Mark's care.) After unlocking and opening the door to start the car, Mark heard a noise...*mew, mew, mew*. Not a cat sound—kitten sounds! He followed the sound to the corner of the garage, where he pulled out a fluffy white kitten with blue eyes...and another...and another! Just then he realized a worker must have entered the garage and briefly left the door open, allowing a mother cat to enter right behind him, give birth to the kittens, and leave. (The mother cat never reappeared.)

Coincidence? Coincidence that the day the mother cat gave birth was also the day Mark went into the garage, not having been there for over three months? Coincidence that after looking all over the city and not finding even one kitten, a pregnant cat crawled out of the bush, climbed over an eight-foot stone wall surrounding the house, and snuck past workers and a big rottweiler instead of giving birth in a less dangerous place?

Or maybe God really does value the prayer of a four-year-old...and the longing of a dad for his daughter to receive a Christmas gift she really wanted.

DISCUSSION OPENERS

1. How do you think Mark felt when he realized his little girl wouldn't receive presents from home for Christmas? Do you think God ever feels that way for us?

2. Can you think of a time when you asked God for something and He provided it miraculously? Tell about it.

3. Breanna asked God for a kitty, a small thing but difficult to come by. Is there a "small thing" you'd like to ask and trust God for today?

4. How can viewing God as your "daddy" in heaven affect the way you pray?

SCRIPTURES FOR GOING DEEPER

Matthew 6:31–33
Matthew 7:11

A PRAYER

Thank You, Father, that You love us so much more
than we love our precious children.
Thank You that Your willingness to answer our prayers
far surpasses our willingness to give good gifts to our children.
When we need something, even though it's something small,
help us remember Your lovingkindness and to ask for it as a child.
In Jesus' name, amen.

A PARTING THOUGHT

"The Father knows that it is in our daily lives that we most easily become anxious. He knows, too, that our daily lives are made up of little things, not great things. Therefore He beckons to us in a friendly way and says, 'Just bring all those little things to me: I am most willing to help you.'"

O. HALLESBY

FOURTEEN

Christmas Card Families

We always thank God for all of you, mentioning you in our prayers.
1 THESSALONIANS 1:2

ome on, girls, it's time for prayers," Karen Wingate called up the stairs to her two daughters. Soon the enthusiastic bounce of not-so-little feet shook the ceiling above her head, and two squirming, pajama-clad bodies still damp from baths nestled beside Mom and Dad.

"Katherine, it's your turn to lead," Karen prompted.

"Daddy...what'syourbestpart...?" their ten-year-old asked, slurring the words together so much that her father could barely understand her.

"Start again and speak more slowly," he admonished.

"Daddy. What's. Your. Best...." Christine, age nine, chimed in with a giggle, trailing off sleepily and putting a pillow over her head.

"Let's get serious, okay?" Karen said. "Remember why we do this. We want to remember the good things that have happened to us so we can thank God for how He has helped us through today."

The two girls settled down, and each family member shared the special moments of the day: shooting a basket in P.E. (something they'd prayed about just the night before), eating a favorite food for supper, playing with a friend after school, and enjoying special, uninterrupted Mom-and-Dad time at a local restaurant. Together, they thanked God for these blessings.

Then, after praying for a piano recital both girls would play in and a math test one of them would take the next day, Karen pulled out a basket filled with Christmas cards. Wanting the girls to learn to pray for others instead of only for themselves, she had decided to use the cards to remind the family to pray for their friends and relatives. Each night they prayed for someone who had sent them a Christmas card the previous year. They then sent that person or family a note saying, "Today we prayed for you."

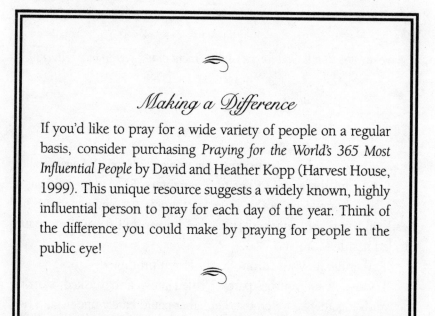

Making a Difference

If you'd like to pray for a wide variety of people on a regular basis, consider purchasing *Praying for the World's 365 Most Influential People* by David and Heather Kopp (Harvest House, 1999). This unique resource suggests a widely known, highly influential person to pray for each day of the year. Think of the difference you could make by praying for people in the public eye!

This night, they pulled out card number eight. They had lots more to go. Karen wondered if the nightly practice would ever get old. She silently prayed, "Lord, help the girls remain enthusiastic about this project. Help us love and intercede for people as You do." Aloud she said, "Our family tonight is David and Lynette."

"Who are they? I don't know them," replied Christine.

"Lynette was a good friend of mine in college. She and David have a new baby boy. They've waited so long for a baby, so we can thank God for their child. I don't think David is a Christian, but their Christmas letter sounds like he's beginning to attend some church activities. Still, let's pray for David's salvation."

As the girls prayed for this family they didn't even know, Karen was astounded at the depth of their prayers. She expected her daughters to focus on the baby; instead they both fervently prayed that David would become a Christian, that he'd have a real encounter with Jesus and experience His love.

As soon as the girls were settled in bed, Karen headed to her computer to print out the special card they'd made for their Christmas card families. So far, they hadn't received any reactions to their efforts to pray for their friends and relatives. But they didn't expect responses; that wasn't the purpose.

So they were pleasantly surprised to receive a handwritten note from Lynette within a week of praying for her family. When the Wingates sat down for devotions that night, Karen read aloud what her friend had written. "The day you prayed for me was my birthday," the note read. "And it was one of the best birthdays I have had in my life." The note concluded, "Please pray for David's salvation."

The girls beamed. "Hooray, God! He helped us pray right on the target!" Christine exclaimed. With renewed enthusiasm the family has continued to pray for David and for other Christmas card families. Often Christine asks whether each person is a Christian. If Mom answers no, the girls focus right on that need.

And while this family has focused on praying for others, they've seen growth in their own lives, especially in their prayer lives. "Our prayers have taught us to focus and think about the deeper needs of those we pray for," says Karen. "It's caused us to thank God for the special blessing various people have been in our lives. I don't think I've ever thanked God for Jo, my 4-H leader of long ago, or for Cora, a dear, older lady who fulfilled her desire to use her car for God's service by carting me and my infant daughter wherever we needed to go."

Their greatest thrill has been hearing the entire family pray in one accord about a specific need for a specific person. Only eternity will bear out the results of those prayers.

DISCUSSION OPENERS

1. The Wingate family's prayer time started with thanking God for His goodness—even the little blessings of the day. That's a good way to enter God's presence. In the psalms David advises us to enter His gates with thanksgiving and His courts with praise. Over and over he writes, "Give thanks to the LORD, for He is good!" What happens when we begin our prayer time this way?

2. Why do we need to pray for the salvation of friends and family members who aren't Christians?

3. The Wingates' prayer huddle took just a brief amount of time from their day. When can your family find time to huddle together in prayer?

SCRIPTURES FOR GOING DEEPER

Ephesians 1:17–19a
Colossians 1:9–12
(These are both wonderful verses to pray for Christmas card families and friends.)

A PRAYER

Lord, You said to seek You first,
but sometimes we're so busy that we find ourselves seeking You last.
Forgive us and help us to love You more
and to love and care about others as we do ourselves.
Help us find time as a family to lift our praises and thanks,
our intercessions and petitions to You
for ourselves and especially for those we love.
In Jesus' name, amen.

A PARTING THOUGHT

"There is no more significant involvement in another's life than prevailing, consistent prayer. It is more helpful than a gift of money, more encouraging than a strong sermon, more effective than a compliment, more reassuring than a physical embrace."

CHARLES R. SWINDOLL

FIFTEEN

The Street Where You Live

When someone becomes a Christian, he becomes a brand new person inside.
He is not the same anymore. A new life has begun!
2 CORINTHIANS 5:17 (TLB)

When Corrie Ten Boom was five years old, she asked Jesus into her life. With a childlike prayer of faith she turned her life over to Him. "It was so simple," Corrie later reflected, "and yet Jesus Christ says that we all must come as children, no matter what our age, social standing, or intellectual background."[1]

From that point on, Jesus became more and more real to young Corrie ten Boom, and she began praying for other people. She had a particular burden to pray for the poor people of Smedestraat, a street of saloons behind her family's house. When she jumped rope outside, little Corrie saw the hopeless drunks slouching in doorways and being arrested by the police. She heard the cries of neglected children on the curb. Her heart broke. As she walked that street to go to school and as she played with friends outside, sometimes she just wept and prayed for the people, asking God to save them and bring them out of darkness into His light. "Dear Jesus, help those men…and Jesus, help all the people on the Smedestraat," she would pray.[2]

Years later as an adult, Corrie took eighteen young women on a campout. As they sat around the fire that night, each girl shared her testimony about how she had come to know Christ as Savior and Lord. As Corrie listened to their stories, she realized that all of the girls or their parents had lived on Smedestraat, the very place where God had first touched her heart to pray every day for people she didn't even know. The Lord had used the prayers of a small child to reach them, and these girls had come out of darkness into God's light. Her prayers had indeed made an eternal difference.

Who's praying for the people on your street?

DISCUSSION OPENERS

1. If God would do one good thing you asked for a person or group of people, what would you ask Him to do? Why not pray that prayer today?

2. How might God be prompting you to pray for the people on your street? In your school or workplace?

3. Do you ever feel too small to pray big prayers? If so, how might Corrie ten Boom's story encourage you?

4. Corrie's experience of accepting Christ happened right at home. While playing house one day, she knocked on a pretend door, and her mother said, "Corrie, I know Someone who is standing at your door and knocking right now." Their ensuing discussion resulted in Corrie opening her heart to Christ. Have you accepted Jesus Christ as your Savior?

5. Prayer isn't always words and sentences. Sometimes, such as in Corrie's childhood experiences, prayer is tears of compassion for someone. How do you feel knowing that God understands as prayers your sighs, groans, tears, and garbled words? (See Romans 8:26–27 for a biblical explanation of this.)

SCRIPTURES FOR GOING DEEPER

Romans 8:26–27
Ephesians 6:18
Colossians 4:2–4

A PRAYER

Lord, make us sensitive to the people who live on our street,
and prompt us to pray for them
so they'll become brand-new people inside.
May Your kingdom come in their lives.
In Jesus' name, amen.

A PARTING THOUGHT

"Never doubt whether God hears our prayers, even the unusual ones. And never doubt that He listens—and responds to the prayers of a child."

CORRIE TEN BOOM

SIXTEEN

Monday:

Praying for Missionaries

Seeing the people, He felt compassion for them,
because they were distressed and dispirited like sheep without a shepherd.
Then He said to His disciples, "The harvest is plentiful, but
the workers are few. Therefore beseech the Lord of the harvest
to send out workers into His harvest."
MATTHEW 9:36–38 (NASB)

*S*ometimes families find it difficult to get into a rhythm of praying together. It may seem an overwhelming undertaking
when you have so many things to pray for—missionaries you
know, neighbors who don't know Christ, friends and family members
who need God's help, your own family's needs—and so little time!

Let's spend the next five devotions "spying" on a family that has
found a manageable way to cover a lot of bases in prayer. Every morning after breakfast, the Sjogren (pronounced "show-grin") family has a
five-minute intercession time. As you'll see in the pages ahead, they
focus on a different prayer category each day of the week. On Monday,
they pray for missionaries; on Tuesday, for two friends. Wednesday is
Witnessing Day; Thursday is Thankful Day; and Friday is Family Day.

Let's join the Sjogrens as they pray Monday morning...

Debby picked up the cereal bowls and banana peels as she scooped her four-year-old out of his chair. She turned to Luke, Abby, and Elise, ages ten, nine, and seven. "It's Monday…so why don't you three go to the map and pick the photo of the missionary you want to pray for today. I'll be right over. And Luke, would you check our e-mail to see if we've received messages from any of the families?"

The Sjogrens' five-minute intercession time was as much a daily habit as eating breakfast. For that brief period, Debby and her four children interceded for a missionary selected from the photos attached to their world map.

As Debby finished clearing the table, the girls picked the photo of Steve Joseph, a missionary to an unreached group of Middle Eastern Muslims, while Luke turned on the computer. As he accessed the family's e-mail, Luke found an emergency e-mail from Steve's family.

"Mom," Luke said, reading from the screen, "it says Mr. Steve's been sick for several months with respiratory problems, and a recent doctor's exam showed he was only using forty percent of his lung capacity. They might have found a spot on his lung. And they're flying back to the U.S. immediately to have a specialist diagnose the problem. The situation is grave and serious. We've got to pray for him!"

Steve Joseph, his wife, and his two children had stayed in the Sjogrens' home for several weeks when in the U.S. The two families had shared meals together, laughed together, and played together. Even though the Joseph family lived across the world, the Sjogren children felt close to them. The Sjogrens also knew that the Josephs were key missionaries in that area of the world; the Josephs knew the language well and had already started one church in a nearby region.

"Father God, please touch and heal Mr. Steve's body so he can continue serving You," Luke prayed.

"And Lord, be with his wife and children so they won't be afraid while their daddy is sick," Elise petitioned.

"Jesus," Abby prayed, "please touch Mr. Steve with Your healing hand."

"God, don't forget the Muslim people the Josephs were reaching out to while they have to be out of the country. Please continue to somehow send Your love to them," Debby interceded.

Although Monday is the Sjogrens' Missionary Day for their morning prayer time, after the emergency e-mail they continued interceding daily for this man and his family until they heard the test results. Luke took a special interest in Steve's illness and even wrote an e-mail to tell Steve he was praying for him.

A week later, another e-mail arrived. The doctors in Washington had diagnosed a lung problem, probably because Steve's office was located above a shoe factory. Breathing the glue fumes every day had caused a severe reaction in his respiratory system, but it was not life threatening as they had originally thought. And instead of having to wait six to twelve months to return to their Middle Eastern mission post, the Josephs could leave within a month.

When Luke saw the report, his face lit up with joy. "Wow! Thank You, God!"

Debby, Luke, Abby, Elise, and even Hunter, the four-year-old, were overjoyed at the news. Once again, they had seen God do something wonderful when they prayed. Little by little, the children were learning that though they were young, their prayers made a difference!

DISCUSSION OPENERS

1. Why is it important to pray for missionaries as the Sjogren family did?

2. As a family, which missionaries can we pray for? What time can we set aside to pray for them?

3. Although God calls some of us to stay home and support missionaries financially and with our prayers, He calls others to go to the fields that are ripe for harvest. What about you? What has God called you to do now...and in the years to come?

SCRIPTURES FOR GOING DEEPER

Psalm 2:8
Acts 4:10, 12
James 5:16

A PRAYER

Heavenly Father, thank You for our brothers and sisters in Christ
who answer Your call to missions.
Give us hearts that desire to share their burden
by praying that Your Kingdom will come and Your will would be done
even to the ends of the earth. And now we pray for:
(missionaries you know)
In Jesus' name, amen.

A PARTING THOUGHT

"The great need of missions is the obtaining of men and women who will give themselves to the Lord to strive in prayer for the salvation of souls. God is eager and able to deliver and bless the world He has redeemed, if His people were but willing, if they were but ready, to cry to Him day and night."

ANDREW MURRAY

Making a Family Prayer Plan

Here's a quick overview of the Sjogren's Five-Days-a-Week, Five-Minute Intercession Plan and ways to put it into practice in your own family:

Monday   *Praying for Missionaries*—Collect photos of missionary families and place the photos in a basket or tack them to a world map on the countries where the families serve (hang the map where your family will see it often). Every Monday have your kids choose photos from the basket or the map and pray for the families in those photos.

Tuesday	*Praying for Two Friends*—Have everybody pray for two friends.
Wednesday	*Praying to Witness*—Have everyone pray for a neighbor or friend who doesn't know Christ or a people group or nation that needs to hear the gospel.
Thursday	*Praying with Thankful Hearts*—Have everyone offer a prayer of thanksgiving. If you wish, give each person a "Thankful Book," a blank book for writing or drawing things for which that person is thankful. Give everyone time to write or draw their thanks, then have each person share his or her thanks with the rest of the family.
Friday	*Praying for Family*—Offer prayers for immediate and extended family. You might want to fill a basket with three-by-five cards and pens, and on Friday, set out the basket and invite everyone to write prayer requests on the cards. Then collect the cards, shuffle them, and pass them out. Have each family member pray for the request on the card he or she has received.

If you'd like to continue praying during the weekend, you can designate Saturday and Sunday as days to pray for your pastors and your church.

Praying for People in the 10/40 Window

The 10/40 Window is the area of the world located between ten and forty degrees latitude, which is north of the equator and extends from the tip of North Africa east to Japan. Almost half the world's population lives in that zone, and most of them are Muslim, Hindu, or Buddhist.

- *Why?* Acts 4:10, 12—If Jesus truly is the only way to live with the Father for all eternity, then we must care for, pray for, give to, and send laborers (or go ourselves) into the most needy areas of the world today.
- *How?* Matthew 9:36—When Jesus saw the multitudes of people He had compassion on them, and today we can find multitudes of people within the 10/40 Window. Learn about that area of the world and its needs, look at photos of the people there, or host an international student from that area in your home so you, too, can feel God's compassion for the people of that region.
- *What?* Matthew 9:38; John 4:35—Pray two things for the 10/40 Window: (1) that God's Spirit would move in the people's hearts to make them "ripe for harvest," and (2) that God would "send out workers into His harvest field."
- *Finally, believe!* Isaiah 55:10–12—God promises that when His Word goes out, it will not return to Him empty. As the Holy Spirit prepares hearts and as laborers take the gospel to the people, God will accomplish His desires and purposes. And there will be much joy in all of His creation!

Debby and Bob Sjogren

SEVENTEEN

Tuesday:
Praying for Two Friends

It will also come to pass that before they call, I will answer; and
while they are still speaking, I will hear.
ISAIAH 65:24 (NASB)

oday's devotion is the second in a series of five describing one family's morning practice of interceding for others. Yesterday we read how the Sjogren family prayed for missionaries every Monday morning. Today, let's find out what happens as each family member faithfully prays for two friends every Tuesday.

Luke always looked forward to Tuesday morning prayers because the family designated that day for praying for two friends. While Abby prayed for Kelsey and Whitley and Elise prayed for Cathy and Rachel, Peter topped Luke's list.

Luke met Peter in preschool when they both were four years old, and the two boys had become best friends. But after Peter's parents placed him in a private school and Luke's mom began homeschooling him and his sisters, the two boys had lost touch with each other.

When Luke entered fourth grade, his parents decided to send the children to a newly formed charter public school. Peter's parents did the same thing, and the two boys were assigned to the same class.

And even better, Peter will live with God in heaven forever! God used a child's prayers to make an eternal difference in a friend's life.

DISCUSSION OPENERS

1. How did Luke's friendship with Peter pave the way for Peter to come to Christ?

2. Do you have a friend who doesn't have a personal relationship with God? How can you make it a habit to pray that your friend will accept Jesus Christ?

3. If you have a friend who already knows Christ as Savior, what other things can you pray for him or her?

SCRIPTURES FOR GOING DEEPER

Matthew 7:7–8

John 15:7

A PRAYER

Father God, we pray for these friends to know You:
(insert their names here).
Please reveal Yourself to them
and open their eyes so they can see how much You love them.
Help them accept Your precious gift of eternal life
and Your amazing grace for living each day.
In Jesus' name, amen.

A PARTING THOUGHT

"Prayer avails for the conversion of others. There are few converted in this world in any other way than in connection with someone's prayers.... Oh, the power of prayer to reach down, where hope itself seems vain, and lift men and women up into fellowship with and likeness to God! It is simply wonderful! How little we appreciate this marvelous weapon!"

R. A. TORREY

Again, Luke and Peter became fast friends. Both boys loved sports and just lived for recess when they could play football, soccer, or basketball together. Peter and Luke also played on the same team in the community basketball league.

Luke knew Peter was experiencing a rough time at home and problems at school. One day Peter was bragging about all the cool things his dad had bought him since his dad had moved out, and Luke replied, "Wow, I wish my dad would do that for me...."

"No, Luke," Peter corrected him, "you have it so much better because your dad really spends time with you and doesn't yell at you."

Every Tuesday for several months, Luke prayed for his best friend: "Father God, please open Peter's heart. Help him come to know Jesus as his Savior and Lord. And please heal his parents' marriage, and let his dad come to know you, too."

After Luke began interceding for Peter every week, he decided to invite Peter to his Wednesday night AWANA club at church. Peter tried it, liked it, and began attending regularly. Since Peter's parents were separated, they often asked Luke's mom to bring Peter to Luke's house after school so Peter could attend AWANA more easily. Peter really enjoyed hanging out with the Sjogrens.

Soon Peter received his AWANA handbook and began to memorize some Scripture verses. One night at AWANA he was reciting Ephesians 2:8–9 to Bob (Luke's dad and one of the club leaders) who asked Peter, "Do you know what it means to have faith in Christ for salvation, the gift of new life in Him?"

Bob shared how much Jesus loved Peter and asked, "Peter, have you ever asked Jesus into your life as your Savior and Lord?"

"No," Peter answered.

"Well, would you like to right now?"

"YES!" So with Bob—and Luke—right there, Peter asked the Lord Jesus into his heart. Over the months that followed the Sjogrens slowly began seeing wonderful changes in Peter's life and attitudes. He began to show more self-control. He was getting into less trouble at school. He was able to lose football games without blowing up. His heart softened as he grew in the Lord and began attending church with his mom.

EIGHTEEN

Wednesday:
Praying for the World

And the prayer offered in faith will make the sick person well;
the Lord will raise him up. If he has sinned, he will be forgiven.
JAMES 5:15

oday's devotion is the third in our journey with the Sjogren family through a week of prayer. Let's see what God does through their Wednesday prayers, which focus on people who don't know Christ. (If you're flipping through this book and just happened to open to this page, you might want to read the previous two devotions to understand what we're doing.)

When the Sjogrens moved to Arizona, they no longer lived near a university where they could easily reach out to international students. Instead, they moved into an "all-like-us" suburban neighborhood. Wanting to continue to impact the world for Christ, they began to pray for some way to build relationships with people from other countries.

Soon they realized that someone had removed the For Sale sign from the house next door. One morning the kids were playing outside when they caught a glimpse of four young people carrying boxes, clothing, and a computer into that house. "Mom, Mom!" they called to Debby. "Come and meet the new people on the block. It looks like

God's answered our prayers!" Soon all the Sjogrens met their four new neighbors, one Korean and three Taiwanese students who would commute to Arizona State University.

Debby brought the students homemade bread and, before long, invited them to dinner. The Sjogrens also hosted an open house so the students could meet the other neighbors. Thus began a growing friendship between the Asian students and the Sjogren family. The three men and one woman often joined the Sjogrens for cookouts and other meals and shared Thanksgiving and Christmas dinners with them. And for months the Sjogrens prayed for those students—all of whom were Buddhists—on Wednesday, the day they prayed to witness to others.

Developing a Vision for the World

Even when your children are very young, you can begin developing in them the desire to pray for people around the world. Here's a simple suggestion. After dinner, pull out a brightly colored globe and place it on the table. Let each of your young children take a turn spinning the globe and stopping it with his or her finger. If necessary, help your child say the name of the country where his or her finger has landed. Then encourage your child to say a prayer for people in that country, praying however he or she feels led.

By doing a simple prayer activity such as this one, you help your children realize that the world is much bigger than just your house, neighborhood, school, or church—and that God loves the whole world and wants all people to come to Him.

One day, Con Chen, one of the Taiwanese students, came to Debby to show her a suspicious-looking lump on his neck. He complained of a debilitating headache that had persisted for several days and made him so sick he couldn't sleep or eat. He was worried and in a lot of pain.

The Sjogrens helped Con Chen find a doctor and make an appointment. They also asked if they could pray for him. Eager for any relief, Con Chen agreed. They all sat down in the living room, and the four children gently placed their hands on Con Chen and prayed. Immediately, his headache left! He was amazed at how much better he felt. Later, he came over to say how happy he was that they had prayed for him. When doctors examined the lump on his neck, they said it was nothing to worry about and would dissolve on its own.

A week after the Sjogrens prayed for Con Chen, he appeared at their door with a magnificent Chinese feast—including shark fin soup that the children enthusiastically ate. As the family enjoyed the meal, they shared with Con Chen the good news of Jesus Christ. The young man was more open to the conversation than he had ever been before.

Seeds were planted, and the Sjogrens continued to pray for Con Chen and his housemates, hopeful that someday those students would turn to the God who loves them with an everlasting love.

DISCUSSION OPENERS

1. Why did the Sjogrens pray for Con Chen when he was sick with a headache? (See James 5:13–18.) How do you think he felt inside when they helped him locate a doctor and then asked permission to pray for him?

2. Why did they pray for their neighbors to know Christ even though the students already had their own religion?

3. What is God's wonderful promise if we pray for people of other nations? (See Psalm 2:8.)

4. Do we know anybody from another part of the world who might need to hear about Christ? If so, how can we incorporate praying for these people into our routine? If not, how should we pray so God gives us opportunities to witness to the world?

SCRIPTURES FOR GOING DEEPER

Psalm 2:8

Psalm 67

Psalm 107:19–20

A PRAYER

Lord, give us a heart for the nations,
for people of all races and languages everywhere to know You.
But let us not forget to pray for the lost who live
right in our own neighborhood.
Help us love them just as You do, for You died for them, too.
May they know You and Your love for eternity.
In Jesus' name, amen.

A PARTING THOUGHT

"Our lives should be according to our Lord's plans—quiet but steadily flowing streams of blessing, which through our prayers and intercessions should reach our whole environment."

O. HALLESBY

NINETEEN

Thursday:
Praying with Thankful Hearts

Always giving thanks to God the Father for everything,
in the name of our Lord Jesus Christ.
EPHESIANS 5:20

This is perhaps my favorite day in the Sjogrens' five-day prayer plan. When we focus for a whole day on praising God and thanking Him for His goodness, our cups overflow with joy. Let's tune into Thursday morning at the Sjogren house....

Let me speak to you parents for just a moment. Moms, don't you love your day in May—and dads, your day in June—when your kids give you little gifts and cards that say "I love you, Mommy," and "I love you, Daddy"? Not a card that asks, "Would you get me new Air Jordans?" or "Would you buy me a new outfit?" but one that says, "Thanks for all you do. You're a great mom [or dad]!" How those expressions of gratitude warm the heart of a parent!

Now imagine how God might enjoy it if we took a day to express our love and gratitude to Him—a Heavenly Father's Day. Most of us do designate one day of the year, Thanksgiving, to thank God for our blessings between bites of turkey and dressing and pumpkin pie. But

Thanksgiving should be more than a November day. We can be grateful on a regular basis if we make time to thank God instead of just asking Him for things.

That's what the Sjogrens do every Thursday (Thankful Thursday). During their five-minute prayer time, they don't make requests; they don't pull out their prayer lists or select missionaries or friends to pray for. Instead, they thank God. That's all—they praise and thank Him for their blessings and answered prayers. (I have a feeling the Lord especially looks forward to that time every week.)

Each of the Sjogren children has a Thankful Book, and on Thursday mornings after breakfast, they open their books to record what they're grateful for. Even before the kids could write, Debby encouraged them to draw pictures of their blessings because God understands and receives those expressions of love, too. After everyone has finished writing or drawing, they share their thanksgivings with each other.

At age five, Abby drew three pictures one day and dictated three captions to her mom. "I'm thankful for Jesus because He died on the cross"; "This is me!" to go next to a picture she drew of herself; and "I'm NOT thankful for Satan!" By age six, Abby could write her own narration for her pictures: "I'm thankful for Mom and Dad, that they love each other" beside a picture she drew of her parents kissing. Another day she drew a picture of her new best friend and wrote, "Thank you, Jesus, for answering my prayer and giving me someone to have fun with and go with to church activities!"

At age six, Elise wrote, "God, I'm thankful you keep us safe frum fires and frum toranoradoes" next to a few pictures depicting those disasters. (I don't think God worried one moment about little Elise's misspellings.) At age seven Elise wrote, "Thank you, God, for tello phones, without them we could not talk to our frends" and drew a picture of her uncle in Ohio talking by phone with her in Arizona. The next week she wrote, "I thank you, God, for spiders. Without them the flys would bug us" next to a lovely picture of a spider in her web.

At age eight, Luke wrote, "I am thankful for the many years, months, days, hours, minutes, and seconds that we get to live!" Two years later he was really into sports and wrote, "I thank You, Heavenly Father, for letting my basketball team win another game. And thank you for Hunter, the brother I asked for so long ago!" (Hunter is Luke's younger brother by five years. He had prayed for a brother because he already had two sisters!)

Little by little, as time has passed and the children have faithfully thanked God every Thursday for His blessings big and small—His protection, friends, telephones, basketball wins, answered prayers, sunshine-filled days, rainbows, and much more—an attitude of gratitude and joy has grown in their hearts. Even when life seems hard or the kids face a string of difficulties, they look for the positive stuff. They notice the little things God does for them and quickly express their thanks. And gratitude and praise spills over into their prayers during the rest of the week so they can readily "enter His courts with thanksgiving."

The children's Thankful Books serve another purpose, too. As the kids record the tangible things God does in their lives, they develop a personal history of His faithfulness. As the days go by, they can look back and see not only how their drawing and spelling has improved, but how their relationship with God has grown.

And that's something else to be thankful for!

DISCUSSION OPENERS

1. What good things did the children experience as they regularly gave thanks to God on Thankful Thursday?

2. James 1:17 says that every good gift we receive comes from God. That includes every good meal, every beautiful sunrise, every favorite pet , every toy, every birthday present, every hug and expression of love from our parents, every fun activity we do, and every breath we take! Take some time right now to thank God for all the wonderful things He has given you.

3. Second Corinthians 9:15 says, "Thanks be to God for His indescribable gift!" meaning Jesus Christ. Have you thanked God lately for sending His Son so we could receive His forgiveness and enjoy abundant life here on earth and eternally in heaven?

SCRIPTURES FOR GOING DEEPER

>1 Chronicles 16:34
>Psalm 92:1
>1 Thessalonians 5:18

A PRAYER

Thou hast given so much to me. Give one thing more—a grateful heart:
Not thankful when it pleaseth me,
as if Thy blessings had spare days,
but such a heart whose pulse may be Thy praise.

GEORGE HERBERT

A PARTING THOUGHT

"If you discern God's love in every moment of happiness, you will multiply a thousandfold your capacity to fully enjoy your blessings."

FRANCES J. ROBERTS

Developing an Attitude of Gratitude

When we parents teach our kids to be grateful, we give our children a great tool for spiritual and emotional health. Even secular psychologists proclaim the enormous benefits of expressing gratitude both to God and to people who bless us; it shifts our minds from negative thought patterns to more healthy, balanced attitudes. Gratitude helps us put problems in perspective and gives us hope.

To give your kids the gift of gratitude, promote thankfulness in your home. You might choose to set aside a Thankful Day during the week as the Sjogrens have, or you can inaugurate your own creative method for stirring up thankfulness. Here are some suggestions to get you going:

- Put a "Blessings Basket" in the middle of the dinner table, with slips of paper and pens in it. Have everyone in the family take a pen and a slip of paper from the basket and jot down (or draw a picture, if kids can't yet write) the blessings they experienced during the day or past week. Then have everyone share what he or she wrote. Keep the lists in the basket for future reference.
- At bedtime, ask each child, "What are two things about your day for which you're grateful?" then thank God together for those happy moments. Encourage your child to say a prayer of thanks whenever he or she experiences something good because every good gift comes from God!
- Take a walk to a nearby park, lake, or forest, and thank God for each bit of His creation that you see: trees, animals large and small, blue sky, rocks, and other "nature finds."

TWENTY

Friday:
Praying for Family

I love the LORD, because He hears My voice and my supplications.
Because He has inclined His ear to me,
Therefore I shall call upon Him as long as I live.
PSALM 116:1–2 (NASB)

If you've spent the last four devotions with us, following the Sjogrens as they pray five minutes each weekday morning, then you know we're ready to see how they pray on Fridays, the day they set aside to pray for family needs, both within their immediate family and among their extended family.

Nine-year-old Abby missed her friends. She had lived in Arizona ever since she was born, but now her family had moved all the way across the United States to Virginia, and she was having trouble making new friends.

Hoping Abby would connect with some girls at church, her parents encouraged her to attend the Wednesday night group where forty girls her age gathered for fellowship and Bible teaching. But for the several weeks Abby had attended the group, she sat at a table alone with hardly anyone talking to her. She felt lonely, embarrassed, and sad.

So one Friday morning, the day the Sjogrens pray for family needs,

Abby asked for prayer. Her mom pulled out the Prayer Box, which held three-by-five cards for prayer requests and answered prayers. Abby wrote her need on a card: "God, I need a best friend—soon—and some way to begin to feel at home." After each of the children had written their requests, Debby collected the cards, shuffled them, then passed them out. One by one, the children petitioned God for His help and provision for each need, especially Abby's need for a friend.

A few weeks after they began praying for Abby, her Wednesday night teacher, Mrs. Beasley, discovered that Abby lived down the street from her house. Mrs. Beasley had a daughter Abby's age, Katy. One day Katy asked Abby over to play. A couple days later Abby invited Katy over to her house. Before long Abby and Katy were close friends.

As the girls spent time together, Mrs. Beasley noticed Abby's flair for the dramatic. She asked Abby to be a "reporter" for the Wednesday night group, interviewing interesting adults from the church in front of the girls. So Abby began conducting live, in-person interviews using questions Mrs. Beasley had prepared; she enjoyed it and so did the other girls. One week Mrs. Beasley forgot the interview questions, so Abby ad-libbed and kept the whole group in stitches. Her role as reporter broke the ice for her and she became acquainted with many of the other girls in the class. Now Abby felt accepted and at home—not just in the neighborhood but also at church.

The next Friday, Abby joyfully wrote a big "AP!" (the family code for Answered Prayer) in red marker on her prayer request card and dropped it in the Prayer Box. God had not only answered her need, He had done more than she could have asked or imagined.

DISCUSSION OPENERS

1. What two specific things did Abby pray for? E. M. Bounds wrote that when our asking is specific, God's answering is also specific—meaning that the Lord *wants* us to pray for specific needs instead of just asking for general blessings.[1] What would you like to specifically request from God today?

2. Why or how did Abby acknowledge that God, not coincidence, had given her newfound friendships and an "at home" feeling? What

prayers has God answered for you lately?

3. What are some needs within our family—both our immediate family and our extended family—that we can pray for today?

SCRIPTURES FOR GOING DEEPER

Psalm 91:15

Matthew 7:11

Ephesians 3:20–21

A PRAYER

Lord, You are so gracious to answer our prayers.
You know our needs and the secret places
of hurt and discouragement that need Your touch.
You never tire of seeing us come to Your throne of grace;
You welcome us to pray over and over so You can show us again and again
that You hear and answer the prayers of Your children.
What a loving Father You are!
In Jesus' name, amen.

A PARTING THOUGHT

"Answered prayer is the spring of love, and is the direct encouragement to pray."

E. M. BOUNDS

TWENTY-ONE

When God Says Wait

The Lord is good to those who wait for Him,
To the person who seeks Him.
LAMENTATIONS 3:25 (NASB)

Have you ever prayed for something, prayed really hard, yet the answer you wanted didn't come when you wanted it?

If so, then you probably understand Zachary's frustration.

As a preschooler, Zack fashioned little bows and arrows from sticks and string. He imagined himself as Robin Hood, performing all sorts of daring exploits with sturdy weapons. But by the time Zack turned six years old, he had grown tired of the "play" bows and arrows. He wanted the real thing!

So Zack asked his parents for a real bow and arrows. He was sure he could handle them, but his parents weren't. After all, their six-year-old was asking for a five-pound compound bow with sharp arrows. And Zack's mom and dad were concerned about his safety and the safety of his younger siblings, Nicholas and Kathryn.

"But Mom, I can learn how to use the bow. I'm big now," Zack pleaded. As the oldest kid in the family, he did feel pretty big. "I'll be careful!"

"We think you're too young for an adult-size bow and arrows," his mom said. "Stick with your karate for now, and we'll see about it later."

This reply didn't satisfy Zachary. He wanted a bow and arrows *now!*

So he kept asking, pleading, begging. Whenever he and his parents went into the sports store, he rushed to the archery center and gazed longingly at the compound bows. He tried talking his dad into buying one for him, but to no avail.

Zack whined and bugged his mom until she was worn out. So she finally said, "You need to pray about this. We don't feel you're old enough. Why don't you ask God and see what He says."

So Zack took his request to the Lord during his bedtime prayers. Surely God would have an opinion different from that of Mom and Dad. But after some pretty serious prayer over several evenings, Zack distinctly heard the Lord say in His still, small, unmistakable voice, "Just wait a little bit."

After hearing God's words, Zack didn't pressure his mom anymore. He became interested in swimming, science experiments, and magic tricks, and the years passed rapidly. As Zack approached his ninth birthday, his parents watched him develop new interests and grow in responsibility. He had also begun trusting their wisdom and obeying them more. His mom and dad didn't say anything about it to him, but they were beginning to feel Zack could handle the big bow.

On Zack's ninth birthday, he received a surprise. When he walked into the kitchen for breakfast that morning, the compound, grown-up bow he had always wanted was sitting in his chair! His dad set up bales of hay and targets in the backyard by the fence where Zack now practices when no one is in the yard.

Someone once said that when God is the most silent He's cooking up the best surprises. And like Zack's parents, God often waits until we're ready before giving us something we want. He always reserves the best for us when we want His will more than our way.

Catherine Marshall writes, "Waiting plays an enormous role in the unfolding story of God's relationship to man...but we have such trouble getting *our will, our time schedules* out of the way" (Marshall's emphasis). Much of the time, she says, we act like a child who brings a broken toy to his father to mend. The father gladly takes the toy, beginning the work right away. Then after a while, the child's impatience takes over as he wonders, *Why is it taking so long? Why isn't my toy fixed?*

The child stands by, getting his hands in the father's way, offering a lot of meaningless advice and some rather silly criticism. Finally in desperation, the child grabs the toy from the father's hands and walks off with it, saying rather bitterly that he hadn't really thought his father could fix it anyway. Perhaps it wasn't even "his will" to mend toys.

But, Marshall's analogy continues, when we trust God enough to leave our "broken toy"—our problem, request, or need—in His hands, He returns it to us restored and fixed and with an added benefit: while we waited, resting from our efforts and allowing God to handle things, we grew spiritually, becoming more patient, more able to hear God's voice and obey.[1]

But what about when we pray for someone who has cancer, wanting her to live, and she dies several weeks later? If God reserves the best for that person when we ask for good, we have to remember that death is not the booby prize. If that person is a Christian, it's graduation time, the ultimate healing!

Deuteronomy 29:29 says, "The secret things belong to the LORD our God" (NASB). Often we don't understand what God is doing. Whether He says wait or even an outright no, we might feel perplexed. But ultimately it boils down to trust, believing that God has our best at heart.

Like Zack's parents, God wants to give us good gifts *when we're ready*. And often, waiting steers us to God's higher and better purposes for our lives.

DISCUSSION OPENERS

1. Read aloud Joseph's story (Genesis 37; 39–46:7) in a children's Bible or an easy-to-read translation such as the New Living Translation. How did Joseph's character grow during his waiting years? What great things did God accomplish through Joseph as he waited?

2. What are some of the qualities God develops in us as we wait for His answers to prayer?

3. Are you waiting for God to answer a prayer? If so, how might God be using the waiting time to prepare you for His answer?

4. How can the family encourage you to continue to wait and pray for what you want?

SCRIPTURES FOR GOING DEEPER

Psalm 37:34
Isaiah 40:31
Isaiah 55:9

A PRAYER

Lord, we are so impatient.
We often want things before Your timing is right,
and sometimes we even think we know better than You do.
Forgive us, and help us to trust Your love and plan in our waiting times
because Your time is better than our time
and Your ways higher than our ways.
As we wait, develop in us patience, love, and faithfulness,
and prepare us for all You have planned.
In Jesus' name, amen.

A PARTING THOUGHT

"There are good things God must delay giving until the child has a pocket to hold them—until he gets his child to make that pocket. He must first make him fit to receive and to have. There is no part of our nature that shall not be satisfied—and that not by lessening it, but by enlarging it to embrace an ever-enlarging enough."

GEORGE MACDONALD

TWENTY-TWO

Getting Out of the Ruts of Prayer

"But we will devote ourselves to prayer and to the ministry of the word."
ACTS 6:4 (NASB)

Melissa, her husband Tony, and her daughters Megan and Emma reverently bowed their heads for dinnertime prayer. At least, Melissa *thought* they were being reverent.

"God, thank You for this food and for giving me a job so I can provide it," Tony prayed. "Thank You for our day. Watch over Emma and Megan in their power tumbling classes tonight, and watch over Melissa as she drives them to school and all their activities. And we pray for those people who don't have any shelter tonight. Give us Your guidance and help us through another day...."

Just as her husband was about to say Amen, Melissa peeked out of one eye and saw twelve-year-old Megan looking straight at her sister, struggling to hold back laughter. Emma had her face in her plate, chomping away at the pepperoni and cheese pizza.

Mom started to scold Emma, but chuckles overtook everyone at the sight of Emma's face covered with tomato sauce. After the silliness subsided, the parents tried to explain to both girls the importance of talking to God.

"It's just boring, Mom. We always say the same things," Megan said.

"Besides, I was hungry!" Emma chimed in.

Tony and Melissa wanted prayer to become a vital part of the girls' lifestyle. But their disinterest in prayer made Melissa think. Maybe they were bored with prayer because the family was somewhat inconsistent in doing it. And when they did say grace, they did it exactly the same way every time. Maybe the family needed to get out of the ruts of prayer.

As Melissa searched the Bible for information about prayer, she found that people didn't pray only at the dinner table but in many different places: on mountain tops (Exodus 19:18–19), in caves (1 Kings 19:9–10), at sea (Jonah 2:1–9), on rooftops (Acts 10:9), and in the Temple (Luke 1:8–10). God's people also prayed in dangerous places where they *really* needed His help, such as battlefields (Exodus 17:10–13) and fiery furnaces (Daniel 3:19–27).

Melissa also found that people in the Bible prayed at different times of day and in different ways, such as with hands raised (Psalm 28:2) and on their knees (Luke 22:41). They shouted prayers (Joshua 6:16–20) and sometimes expressed prayers without words (1 Samuel 1:12–16). She realized that, though God did urge us to "pray continually," He never intended that we pray the same way all the time.

From that point on, Melissa looked for different ways for the family to pray. Sometimes they sang the evening blessing, sometimes they knelt, and sometimes they held hands. Sometimes they each said a conversational, sentence prayer thanking God for something good that had happened that day. One night Melissa filled a basket with all the valentines the girls received from their classroom parties, placed it on the table, and announced that each family member would choose one valentine and pray for the person who gave it. Melissa started initiating spontaneous prayer as she drove Emma and Megan to school in the mornings and made a Family Prayer Box where family members could place special requests for her to pray over during her quiet time.

A few months later, Melissa realized that something must have clicked. After a particularly rough day at school, Megan came to the dinner table, grabbed her parents' and sister's hands, and announced, "I want to say a prayer!" She proceeded to pray for Emma's skinned nose to heal quickly, for her dad's job, and for their impending spring break trip. She finished with an earnest plea for God to help her with her homework. Prayer became something the girls looked forward to instead of dreading, and they found that talking to God could be just as much fun as pizza and power tumbling.

Recently baptized together, Melissa's family is growing in Christ as everyone realizes they can talk to God anytime, anywhere, and in many different ways...and that He's always listening.

DISCUSSION OPENERS

1. What's your favorite way to pray? Why?

2. Do we ever get in a rut of prayer as a family or as individuals? Explain.

3. How can we get out of the rut? How can we pray in new and different ways?

SCRIPTURES FOR GOING DEEPER

Read the Scriptures referenced in the story to explore different ways of praying.

A PRAYER

Lord, blow the winds of Your Spirit on our prayer times!
Refresh us with new ways to pray
so we can get out of our ruts
and seek You with wholehearted enthusiasm.
Remind us to pray in the morning, in the night, and all the times in between.
May we never grow tired of talking to You!
In Jesus' name, amen.

A PARTING THOUGHT

"Get out of the ruts of prayer. Some of us can only pray in one way, and consequently we get tired of praying. The ruts of prayer are the deepest ruts in the world. Pray sometimes standing up; then pray kneeling; then pray sitting down; then pray lying down on your couch at night.

Pray in the morning when the sun first streams in at your window. Pray at noonday when you stand up at the lunch counter in some big city. Pray at night when you go to a place of recreation."

W. H. P. FAUNCE

Different Prayers for Different Kids

Want to keep your children excited about talking to God? Then become aware of the ways God has wired each of them uniquely, and flex with their individual styles. Each person in your family connects with God differently, and children innately love variety. Get out of the ruts and try something new. For example, you could use a visual aid such as a world map, or you could make a Prayer Grab Bag filled with photos or memorabilia of people. Change locations; pray while driving or taking a walk. Create a prayer placemat covered with photos to encourage intercession during meal times.

If your children feel that praying aloud is awkward, hold hands as a family, pray silently, then end by having someone read a verse aloud. Or have each person write down two prayer requests; exchange lists in the morning, then pray for each other during the day.

You can also connect kids' interests and prayer. Sports-oriented children can thank God after a win and pray for a good attitude when they lose. Musical children can sing Scripture prayers set to music or make up original song-prayers. Artistic kids love to draw the things they want to say to God, and verbal kids love praying Korean-style, where everyone prays aloud at the same time.

Give your children room and grace to be who God created them to be. Encourage them to try different styles of prayer and watch them take off!

TWENTY-THREE

The Stone Bearers

Great is the LORD, and highly to be praised,
And His greatness is unsearchable.
One generation shall praise Your works to another,
And shall declare Your mighty acts.

PSALM 145:3–4 (NASB)

The morning sun hung low in the sky, its light warm and clear, as Benjamin and Elihu broke camp on the final day of their journey. They set out along the dusty road, Benjamin's stride matching his father's. At thirteen, he was almost as tall as his father; soon they would be equals.

As they hiked along, Benjamin once again sneaked a glance at his father's strong face. Even after all these miles, when they could almost feel the land sloping down to the river, he found the journey strange. Just a week ago, he had been preparing for bedtime when his father came to him.

"Benjamin," Elihu said, "tomorrow we'll embark on a journey. We'll be gone for many days. Sleep well, son."

Benjamin was full of wonder. "A journey? But harvesttime is near. Surely we can't go somewhere now!"

His father smiled wryly, "Don't think I haven't thought the same thing. But we must go this year. The fields will just have to wait."

"Where? Why?" But Elihu would say no more. Although his father had said to sleep well, Benjamin couldn't. He lay awake that night wondering what, or where, could be so important that his father would leave his fields. And why did Benjamin have to go along? He wasn't a man yet, hardly more than a grown boy. True, he would turn thirteen soon, but even that wasn't old enough to contribute much strength or help to a man in the prime of his life.

As they walked, Elihu revealed just a bit about their destination. "We're going to the Jordan."

"Why?" Benjamin asked.

"To talk," his father answered.

All this just to stand by a river and talk? By now, though, Benjamin knew his father was determined to remain mysterious, so he didn't waste his breath asking questions. Still, he couldn't help sneaking glances as they walked, hoping his father's face would reveal something. But all he saw was a man resolutely set on a goal. Today they would arrive at their final destination, and at last he would know.

The sun was at midsky when Elihu stopped beside a field and looked around. The land was flat, the fields green and fertile. "I think we're close, but it's been a long time. You stay here. I want to ask that man where to go next." Benjamin watched his father pick his way across the field to where a man toiled beneath the hot sun. Elihu approached the man and asked a question Benjamin couldn't hear. The man stopped and wiped his brow as he listened, then he nodded, raised his arm, and pointed. As his father returned, Benjamin could see the excitement glimmering in his eyes. "I was right. It's just down the road!"

As father and son hiked over a gentle rise, they could hear the sound of rushing water, and then there it was: the Jordan river. The mighty rush of water raced past the banks, looking like it might overflow any minute. Benjamin watched as Elihu walked to the edge of the bank, leaned with his hand on a tree trunk, and stared at the rushing water.

"Jehovah be praised," Elihu breathed softly, gazing far into the past. Then, collecting himself, he turned to Benjamin and said simply, "It's time. Come."

After Benjamin approached the water's edge, Elihu began. "Benjamin, when I was your age, my father brought me here and told me this story. Now it's my turn to tell you. This is where it happened and the time of year it happened. The river ran just this high when your grandfather was young and strong.

"Benjamin, our ancestors were slaves years and years ago in Egypt. But Jehovah had power and love, and He set them free."

Benjamin listened as his father told the story again. About the slavery and how God sent Moses to the rescue; about the plagues, the Red Sea, and the long, long weary years in the desert; about the pillar of cloud and fire and the manna. Benjamin had heard it all before, but today, beside the Jordan River, the story somehow seemed more real.

"And then came the time when they were finally going to enter the Promised Land," Benjamin's father continued. "Your grandfather told me often how excited they were that morning when the officers told them what was going to happen. 'Wait for the priests,' they said. 'When you see them carry the ark in front of you, then you can follow. But don't get too close; stay about a thousand yards back.'

"Oh, Benjamin, I wish we could have seen it! All those thousands and thousands of people standing across the river, waiting. They were so excited seeing all that water because they had grown up in the desert and had never seen anything like it. Then the priests picked up the ark and walked down the bank to the water. And the instant their feet touched the water,"—Benjamin looked at the water rushing past their feet—"that very minute the water stopped flowing and piled in a heap upriver, by the town of Adam that we passed yesterday." Benjamin imagined the water standing up on itself. *What happened to all the fish?* he wondered.

"Your grandfather and grandmother walked across the bed of that river. And Benjamin, it was *dry*. Not even the smallest mud puddle to step in. They told me dust rose high into the air that day. Imagine, dust rising from the bottom of a riverbed!

"The priests stood in the middle of the river as all the people walked past them. When everyone reached the other side, Joshua pointed straight at your grandfather—the only one from our whole

tribe!—and said, 'God wants you to go to where the priests are standing and pick up a stone. Put it on your shoulder and bring it out of the
riverbed.' Your grandfather was so proud, Benjamin. He remembered
that moment to his dying day. He went back to the middle of the river,
picked the largest stone he could find, heaved it onto his shoulder, and
carried it right out of that river.

"Now come with me." Benjamin followed his father. As they
rounded a bend, his heart leaped. There stood a pile of stones, twelve
in all, round and large.

"Did Grandfather tell you which one he carried?" Benjamin asked.
His father nodded and wordlessly pointed to a gray-flecked stone
halfway up the pile. Breathless, Benjamin reached out and touched it.
It was warm from the sun, smooth under his hand. He tried to imag-
ine it large, cold, and wet as the river flowed over it, grinding it smooth.
Will I someday be strong enough to carry a stone like this? he wondered.

"Benjamin, never forget. Never forget the power and love of your
God who brought us out of Egypt and gave us this land. Never forget
as you harvest your fields. Never forget as you raise your family. Never
forget your God, the God of your fathers."

DISCUSSION OPENERS

1. Imagine yourself as Benjamin standing at the pile of rocks. How
would it feel to touch the rock your grandfather had carried? Why do
you think God wanted rocks placed there?

2. When has God done something mighty in your life? How do
you feel as you remember that?

3. Every family has a story to tell. God is a part of every story
whether we realize it or not, and each story can tell us something about
God. Tell a family story, then ask, "Where is God in this story? Does our
story remind us of any Bible stories, characters, or principles? What
would God have rejoiced over? What would He wish to change? If you
had to build a memorial to that time, what would you build?"

4. What kinds of things can we do today to build memorials to
remind us of how God provided a need or answered a prayer?

SCRIPTURES FOR GOING DEEPER

Deuteronomy 4:9–10
Psalm 61:5b
Psalm 78

A PRAYER

Father, thank You for placing us in Your family,
for giving us the heritage of all those who love Your name.
Help us not to forget the mighty ways You've worked in this family.
We want to remember and tell our children and grandchildren
what You've done, just as the Israelites did.
And always, we want Your praise on our lips:
praise for what You've done, praise for what You're doing,
and praise for what You will do.
In Jesus' name, amen.

A PARTING THOUGHT

"The single most important truth about people is the truth most easily ignored: that we bear the image of God. As image-bearers, we are called to tell his story with our lives."

LARRY CRABB[1]

Building a Memorial

Make your own family "pile of rocks" to remember what God has done for you, using one of the ideas below or an idea of your own:

- Gather some rocks from a stream or river and place them in a glass jar. When God answers a significant prayer or intervenes in your lives, pull a rock from the jar, write the date and a few key words on it, then return the rock to the jar. Place the jar where you'll see it often.
- Designate a shelf as a Memorial Shelf. Place on it items that signify times, places, and situations where you've seen God at work, such as an itinerary from a trip, a flower in a vase, or a photo.
- Keep a Memorial Journal (you can even use the My Family's Prayer History pages in the front of this book) in which you record God's answers to your prayers and interventions in your lives.

TWENTY-FOUR

A Cross-Country Prayer Drive

First of all, then, I urge that entreaties and prayers,
petitions and thanksgivings, be made on behalf of all men....
This is good and acceptable in the sight of God our Savior,
who desires all men to be saved and to come to the knowledge of the truth.
1 TIMOTHY 2:1, 3–4 (NASB)

The sun shone brightly over the looming St. Louis Archway as Henry, Cindy, and their two teenagers, Shari and Josh, held hands and prayed with all their hearts:

"Lord, strengthen our national leaders and the men of our country," Henry prayed. "Bring repentance and revival to the church in America."

"God, forgive us and have mercy on us for allowing the sin of abortion in our country. Bring revival and refresh the hearts of women, drawing them back to You," Cindy petitioned.

"Lord, bring revival among the youth," prayed Shari, sixteen. "Strengthen them so they can reject immorality. Bless my friends back home, make us closer as a family because of this trip, and turn my generation to You, God."

Josh, thirteen, prayed, "Let all the children in America know You, and make it okay for kids to talk to You at school. And Lord, protect us on our trip...and help us find a bathroom *soon!*"

You've probably heard of prayer concerts and prayer walks, but have you ever heard of a "prayer drive"? On June 22, 1998, the Smiths embarked on a cross-country prayer drive, heading west on I-64 from their Virginia home and making their first stop at St. Louis, Missouri. They took a month to drive the nation's highways and byways, their routes and destinations forming the pattern of a giant cross over America. God had assured them He'd guide their route and show them how to pray.

Thirty days and six thousand miles later, the Smiths had collected a treasure chest full of memories and had prayed from Virginia to Wyoming, Minnesota to West Virginia. Here are a few highlights from their journey:

June 23. At a rest stop off I-70 between St. Louis and Kansas City, the Smiths ran into a destitute family. Because of job failure in Chicago, the mom, dad, and four teenagers were traveling to New Mexico to stay with family, but they had run out of money and were low on gas.

The Smiths could have given them money and quickly moved on, but they knew this family would need a lot more help to make the long trip. The Smiths asked if they could pray for them. The ten people from the two families held hands in the rest area and prayed.

"Lord, grant this family Your protection, provision, and a new job for this dad," prayed Henry.

"Father, just as this is a divine appointment, would You give this family more divine appointments, and let each person come to know You, a heavenly Father who cares for them. Please give them peace, God," said Cindy.

"Lord, bless this family," Josh prayed.

"God, help them get back to their family, and help these teenagers to know You and how much You love them," asked Shari.

Then the four sang "Give Thanks with a Grateful Heart" (a song Henry had written) to the family, gave them money, and said good-bye. As the Smiths left the rest area, they continued praying. A holy peace filled their hearts as they sensed that "heaven was watching."

June 24. The Smiths headed north on I-29 through Omaha, Nebraska, to Sioux City, Iowa, and Rapid City, South Dakota, where they stopped to watch buffalo and encountered a "wall cloud"—a massive black cloud that looked like a wall in the sky. In high winds, hail, and hard rain, the Smiths thanked God for His protection. They saw purple lightning and a highway at sunset that looked like a "highway to heaven," glittering gold with the horizon seeming to rise into the sky. After the storm, they enjoyed an incredible rainbow.

June 25. After traveling to Bozeman, Montana, the Smiths toured Mount Rushmore where they saw the flags of many nations and many people groups. They prayed for a spiritual harvest from the nations and prayed for missionaries to reach all people.

July 3. After a week in Yellowstone and the Tetons, the Smiths headed to East Glacier Park, Montana. Driving through Blackfeet and Crow towns as well as reservation lands, they prayed for Native American people. They sensed the oppression there, the poverty, the alcoholism, and the hopelessness. They stayed there on July 4 and counted it a privilege to be among the Indians on the nation's birthday and to pray blessings over them.

The Smiths continued their prayer drive until they returned home on July 20. Each day brought special blessings and assignments for intercession. Time after time, as they kept their eyes and ears open, God showed them what to pray. For example, as they crossed major rivers across America, they were struck by the pollution in every waterway. Realizing this was a good illustration of the widespread moral pollution in our country, they prayed for the airways and the media and against pornography and anything that would pollute our nation and its people.

A prayer drive involves connecting God with all the things you see around you. It includes looking at life as a visual aid to prayer. Maybe we can't unplug from everything for a month as the Smiths did for a cross-country prayer drive, but all of us pass historical markers that signify battlegrounds where lives were lost or government buildings filled with leaders who make decisions that affect us all. We could pray as we drive by hospitals, churches, schools, playgrounds, and jails. As we faithfully pray, someday in heaven we'll understand the full impact of our prayers!

DISCUSSION OPENERS

1. Read Matthew 18:19. What does this verse say about what happens when even a few people agree together in prayer? How does this

apply to a family praying together as the Smiths did? What does God promise when we do this?

2. Where might God want you to take a prayer drive? (Keep in mind that you don't have to take a month to do it. You might go for a day or even just an afternoon.) Brainstorm together about a route and the stops you'll make.

3. The Smiths listened to the destitute family's story and tried to point to God as their help. What made the Smiths open to encountering and encouraging this family? How might God guide you to touch hurting people as you go on a prayer drive—or wherever you might encounter them? What preparations do you need to make to be open to God's nudging?

SCRIPTURES FOR GOING DEEPER

John 10:4
1 Thessalonians 5:16–18
1 Peter 2:9

A PRAYER

Heavenly Father, give us spiritual eyes to see all of life
from Your perspective. Show us the things in our path You want us to pray
for and the situations and problems that break Your heart.
Give us the faith to believe our prayers will make a difference.
In Jesus' name, amen.

A PARTING THOUGHT

"Begin to realize more and more that prayer is the most important thing you do. You can use your time to no better advantage than to pray whenever you have an opportunity to do so, either alone and with others, while at work, while at rest or while walking down the street. Anywhere!"

O. HALLESBY

Prayer Drive Tips

Several years before embarking on the month-long, cross-country prayer drive, Henry and Cindy took their kids and friends on short prayer missions near their home in Richmond, Virginia. At the top of a twenty-two story city hall building, they interceded for city and state government. They prayed at crisis pregnancy centers; the airport; the oldest Masonic lodge in the nation, which once sold slaves from the basement; and a park notorious for drug-dealing and violence. The Smith kids and their friends enjoy jumping out like a SWAT team at key sites and praying together.

Here are some tips the Smiths learned as they went on these prayer drives:

- *Prepare the pray-ers.* Research the sites you will pray for, and share with your family what you've learned. Help your children understand why you need to pray at that particular place; this knowledge will keep them interested and guide their prayers. If you have a friend who knows some historical background, invite him or her to join you and enlighten you along the way.
- *Assure the pray-ers that God is listening.* Remind everyone that God will hear their prayers and that their prayers will make an eternal difference.

- *Encourage everyone to keep eyes and ears open to see and hear from God.* Invite everyone to walk and look around, listen for God, and ask Him, "How do You want me to pray?" When you come together again, ask everyone, "What did God say to you? Did He show you a picture, put a verse of Scripture in your mind, or convict you about something to pray for here?" Then pray according to what everyone has seen and heard from God.

- *Hold back, adults!* Don't pray first if you're the adult or leader. Hold back and let kids pray first. They may take a little longer to process things, but if you give them enough time, they'll pray! Then pray in agreement with them.

- *Be specific.* If you're praying in the legislative chambers of your state congress, for example, have the kids pray for every chair or sit in key leaders' chairs and intercede. If you stop at the governor's mansion, pray for all who go in and out of its gates, for protection and wisdom for the governor, and that he and his family would know Christ more fully. When we pray specifically, God answers specifically!

TWENTY-FIVE

How Do You Explain God?

God is love.

1 JOHN 4:8B

anny Dutton's teacher gave the eight-year-old and his classmates a homework assignment: write an essay explaining what they thought about God. Here's what Danny wrote:

> One of God's main jobs is making people to replace the ones that die so there will be enough people to take care of things on earth. He doesn't make grown-ups, just babies I think, because they are smaller and easier to make. That way, He doesn't have to take up His valuable time teaching them to talk and walk; He can just leave that to mothers and fathers.
>
> God's second most important job is listening to prayers. God doesn't have time to listen to the radio or TV because of this. Because He hears everything, there must be a terrible lot of noise in His ears unless He has thought of a way to turn it off. God sees everything and hears everything and is everywhere which keeps Him pretty busy. So you shouldn't go wasting His time by going over your mom and dad's head asking for something they said you couldn't have.
>
> Jesus is God's Son. He used to do all the hard work like

walking on water and performing miracles and trying to teach the people who didn't want to learn about God. They finally got tired of Him preaching to them and they crucified Him. But He was good and kind like His Father, and He told His Father that they didn't know what they were doing and to forgive them, and God said okay.

His Dad (God) appreciated everything that He had done and all His hard work on earth, so He told Him He didn't have to go out on the road anymore. He could stay in heaven. So He did! And now He helps His Dad out by listening to prayers and seeing things which are important for God to take care of and which ones He can take care of Himself without having to bother God. Like a secretary only more important.

You can pray anytime you want, and they are SURE to hear you because they got it worked out so one of them is on duty all the time.

If you don't believe in God, besides being an atheist, you will be very lonely because your parents can't go everywhere with you, like to camp, but God can. It is good to know He's around you when you're scared in the dark or when you can't swim very good and you get thrown into real deep water by big kids.

But you shouldn't just always think of what God can do for you. I figure God put me here, and He can take me back anytime He pleases. And that's why I believe in God.[1]

How do *you* explain God?

DISCUSSION OPENERS

1. Explain God from your own point of view.
2. How do we form our ideas about God?
3. Share two things that you appreciate most about God.
4. Look up one of the Scriptures for Going Deeper and share what it shows you about God.

5. Where are you in your relationship with God right now? (If you wish, set out paper and pens for family members to draw their answers to this question.)

SCRIPTURES FOR GOING DEEPER

Psalm 139
Exodus 34:6
John 1
John 3:16

A PRAYER

Lord, we want to know You!
Open our eyes to the wonderful things in Your Word and in creation
that reveal who You are.
Teach us Your ways so we can follow them,
and as we grow bigger and older,
help us know You more and more.
In Jesus' name, amen.

A PARTING THOUGHT

"You should always go to church on Sunday because it makes God happy, and if there's anybody you want to make happy, it's God!"

DANNY DUTTON

Alphabet Praise

God has given us an incredible source for getting to know Him: the Bible. Make a fun activity of discovering God's nature by offering Him "Alphabet Praise." Begin by looking in Scripture for an attribute of God that starts with the letter *A*, such as "awesome" or "able." Then move to *B*, then *C*, and so on until you've completed the alphabet (it may take many family gatherings to accomplish this task). Use the words you list as prompts for praising God during your prayer times. I recommend that you begin your prayers with praise; when you first focus on God's greatness, your needs seem much smaller, you remember God is able to fulfill them, and you feel more encouraged!

TWENTY-SIX

Mighty Prayer Partners

Therefore [Jesus] is able to save completely those who come to God through him, because he always lives to intercede for them.

HEBREWS 7:25

All day long through the dust and heat of the battle, Moses sat on the hilltop. The hot wind carried to him the noise of weapons clashing and people yelling—sometimes faint, sometimes strong.

Even though far away, Moses was helping his people fight: when he held up his arms to God, the Israelites beat back the enemy. But when his arms became tired and weak and began to droop, he could see the line of enemy warriors begin to advance. No matter how valiantly the Israelite men fought, if Moses didn't raise his hands to God, his men went down.

Moses' arms became tired. If he had been alone, the battle may have ended badly for the Israelites. But fortunately, Moses wasn't alone. His brother Aaron and his good friend Hur stood with him throughout that long day, holding up his arms, adding their strength to his weakness. In the end, the Israelites conquered the enemy—not because Moses' arms were strong but because God won the victory for and through them.[1]

Our families will not often have to fight wars with our prayers (at least not physical wars). Most of the time, we pray about ordinary, daily things. Even so, just like Moses, we can feel weak and alone when we pray.

That's a common experience. Corrie ten Boom, a woman of God who hid Jews during World War II and survived Nazi concentration camps, spent her long life joining with others to fight spiritual battles through prayer. But one week Corrie felt very alone as she prayed. Scheduled to speak at a church, Corrie reported for a special prayer meeting to lift up her message. But when she entered the room, she realized she was the only person who had shown up! No one had come to pray *with* her—much less *for* her, the special speaker.

Then Corrie read Romans 8:27 ("The Spirit prays for those who love God") and Romans 8:34 ("Christ prays for us"—Phillips). She realized that she wasn't alone after all. Like Moses, she had companions praying with her, only her companions weren't ordinary humans such as Aaron and Hur. As Corrie prayed, both the Holy Spirit and Jesus were praying, too. That made three people gathered together in prayer![2]

You may have a small family, but think what a mighty group you make when you, your family, Jesus, and the Holy Spirit all pray together! We may feel insignificant when we pray, but God has always delighted in doing great things through small, weak people, whether Moses, Corrie ten Boom…or your family!

DISCUSSION OPENERS

1. When your family prays together, how many people are present? (Don't forget to count Jesus Christ and the Holy Spirit!)

2. Have you ever felt too alone to pray for something? What was the situation? What did you do about it? What happened as a result of your actions?

3. How can today's story encourage you the next time you feel that you're praying alone?

SCRIPTURES FOR GOING DEEPER

Romans 8:26–27, 34
Hebrews 13:5b–6

A PRAYER

God, thank You that You are the banner over us,
that Your love and power always cover and protect us.
Thank You, Jesus, and thank You, Holy Spirit, for praying for us.
What a privilege to know You not only stay with us at all times,
but You also constantly plead for us before God!
Please, when we feel small and all alone,
remind us You're near and that You know exactly what to say when we don't.
With the help of our companions, we lift our hands to You.
Thank You for winning our battles for us!
In Jesus' name, amen.

A PARTING THOUGHT

"Jesus Christ carries on intercession for us in heaven; the Holy Ghost carries on intercession in us on earth; and we saints have to carry on intercession for all men."

OSWALD CHAMBERS

TWENTY-SEVEN

God Wants to Use Children

"Let the little children come to me, and not hinder them, for the kingdom of God belongs to such as these...." And he took the children in his arms, put his hands on them and blessed them.

MARK 10:14B, 16

Throughout many of the devotionals in this book, we've seen what happens when a child prays or a family prays. But what happens when a big bunch of kids pray in unison together? I love what David Walters says about this: "God wants to use children. He wants to reveal Himself to them and move through them. We must reject the idea that children should sit on the sidelines when God is at work."[1]

A Texas church found that out when four hundred kids banded together to pray for their children's pastor. Miss Shirley, as the kids called her, had been diagnosed with breast cancer and had to endure radical surgery, radiation, and chemotherapy over a period of months. The children at her church cared deeply for her and didn't want to sit on the sidelines; they wanted to help their pastor on the battlefield of prayer. "Tell us specific ways we can pray," they told their Sunday school teachers.

Miss Shirley saw her ordeal as a window of opportunity for the children to get to know God better and learn more about prayer. So every week the four hundred kids were given prayer updates and requests, and they prayed up a storm. As they did, they saw God's faithfulness and His specific answers to their petitions.

The kids prayed that the chemotherapy or radiation wouldn't make Miss Shirley sick so she would have to miss church; in nine months of aggressive cancer treatment Shirley never missed a day of work. She experienced fatigue, yes, but never the severe nausea or vomiting. Except for the surgery, she was never so flattened that she couldn't continue in her job. Some of the kids prayed for her hair, others for her strength.

The children also prayed for clear roads and no traffic problems or rain during her drives from the church in Fort Worth to her Dallas hospital. (This would be a miracle in itself since the highways were torn up and construction delays were common). For every one of Miss Shirley's thirty-two treatments, the weather was good and roads were amazingly clear to travel....

Except for one day. The sky was pouring rain and flash flood warnings were issued. However, when Miss Shirley left the church to drive to Dallas, the rain suddenly stopped. And a few hours later, when she pulled into the church's driveway after her treatment, the skies started raining again! There was cheering and clapping the next Sunday when the children heard how God had answered their prayers. And when the doctors pronounced her cancer free a year later, the praise that went up in children's church was heard even by those walking by on the street.[2] (Now, that's the kind of prayer team I'd like to have if I'm in a crisis, wouldn't you?)

You don't need to have four hundred children to experience powerful results like this. Just gathering the kids in your neighborhood, homeschool group, or church to pray can be a great start. Two moms can get together with their children for a weekly kids' prayer time, or a Sunday school class of children can gather on the National Day of Prayer for a children's prayer rally. No matter their size or age, "The prayer of a righteous man is powerful and effective" (James 5:16). Just remember, if you gather the kids, God will be there, too!

DISCUSSION OPENERS

1. There are some circumstances so critical (like Miss Shirley's battle with cancer) that you need a whole army of intercessors, a whole "intensive care unit" to pray. Are there any situations or problems you know that need an army of pray-ers to intercede?

2. Why do you think spiritual power can be multiplied when lots of people unite in prayer with a single focus? How could this glorify God?

3. Are there prayer events in your church or community in which both you and your child could participate? Or how could you begin a kids' prayer group? (My book *When Children Pray* has great ideas for leading and equipping a group of young intercessors.)

SCRIPTURES FOR GOING DEEPER

Proverbs 22:6
2 Timothy 3:15
Psalm 8:2

A PRAYER

Lord, I want to welcome and bless the children in my life.
And I do right now
[Say a prayer of blessing and give thanks for each child].
I'm so glad that You always want the little
[and big] children to come to You.
You have provided a way for us to bring them to You with prayer.
Thank You that You have great plans for them now,
and exciting adventures for them in the future.
In Jesus' name, amen.

A PARTING THOUGHT

"There is a cumulative effect in prayer. The focusing of many prayers on one life or on a situation can change defeat into victory."

E. M. BOUNDS

≈

Plan a Children's Prayer Rally

On the National Day of Prayer or another designated day of prayer, organize a children's prayer rally at a park or government building. Some components of the rally might include a time of worship, a musical performance by a children's choir, breaking into small groups to pray for designated people or topics, launching balloons in which the children have placed individual prayer requests, or signing a huge banner with the kids' prayers and Scripture verses to be sent to the appropriate government office.

≈

TWENTY-EIGHT

When God Says No

But as for me, my prayer is to You, O LORD, at an acceptable time;
O God, in the greatness of Your lovingkindness,
Answer me with Your saving truth.

PSALM 69:13 (NASB)

"Oh, look at that house!" Paula Dinkins exclaimed as it rose into view. The family had just returned to Thailand after a two-year home assignment, and within a few hours a coworker had called to say he had just the house for them and would take them to see it.

"Look at the tree and the swing, Mom!" said Titus, the eight-year-old.

As the Dinkinses walked through the two-story, western-style house in the middle of Chiang Mai, a city in north Thailand, they were positive God had provided this house for them. With all the horrible, run-down houses in the city and the difficulty of finding affordable housing for missionaries, this one seemed ideal.

"Look at this, kids, a real fireplace where we can hang your stockings at Christmas!" Paula called to Amber and Titus. The house also had enough bedrooms for the two older boys who would come home from boarding school from time to time. They could use the extra rooms downstairs for hospitality or teaching Bible studies, and the children would have plenty of room to play in the backyard. With the house's location close to mission headquarters and the younger children's school, it couldn't have been more perfect.

As they toured the house and yard, Paula and her family began daydreaming about where to put their belongings. However, as they chatted with the landlady, they soon discovered some disappointing news. She wanted twenty-five dollars more per month than their rent allotment, which was set by the mission. Paula pleaded for a lower price, but the landlady wouldn't budge.

So they went to their supervisor. Perhaps since they needed just a small amount more, he would allot them the extra money. When he said no, they asked if they could take twenty-five dollars from their personal account each month to cover the cost. For three weeks they waited for the organization's decision, all the while staying in a room at the mission's guest house, unable to unpack their barrels or boxes.

The house seemed so right. They were willing to wait. They had prayed about it; surely it would work out. But as the day arrived when they'd know for sure, things didn't look good. They'd heard no to every previous request, and each time they heard it, Paula found herself growing more frustrated. With the scarcity of homes in Chiang Mai, she felt angry about not receiving approval for the house they wanted. She was tired of staying in the small guest house. And besides, they had one of the largest families on the field. She didn't want to stay resentful and be a poor example to her kids, yet she really wanted that house!

"Children, come and pray with me about the house," Paula said. So the three of them knelt by the bed and prayed.

"Dear Jesus, we really like this house, and I could have my own room..." Amber began.

"And we could have people over and play in the tree swing, and thank You, Jesus," Titus chimed in.

"Lord, if this is the house You have for our family, then we thank You for how You are going to work this out." Paula prayed. But then she realized that if things didn't work out, perhaps that house wasn't God's best for them. So she continued to pray: "And if not, then we thank You, also, because You must have something even better. Amen."

Sure enough, when Larry returned, he had bad news: The supervisor had said they couldn't use their own money for the rent. Unless the landlord would reduce the price, they couldn't have the house.

The whole family was sad and disappointed, and they didn't know where to look for another house. Decent rental houses were so scarce.

Then Paula remembered something. "What about the church God brought to my mind before we left?" she asked Larry. For several months before returning to Thailand, she had prayed about the family's return to the mission field, and God had given her a picture in her mind of a church in the northern part of Chiang Mai. They had attended this church only once. In the hubbub of arriving in town and trying to get the other house, she had totally forgotten about it.

The family again thanked God for the closed door, then asked Him about this new possibility. Could God have something else for them? Larry and Paula decided to see. They borrowed a motorcycle and headed for the church. No one was there except for the caretaker, and he didn't know of any houses for rent in that area. Larry and Paula left their name and phone number for the pastor just in case and jumped back on the motorcycle. Just as they turned toward the main road, Paula noticed a small For Rent sign.

They pulled over and gazed at a two-story house with a small yard and carport. Paula memorized the phone number on the sign, and they hurried back to the guest house to call the landlord. Unfortunately, the landlady wanted two hundred dollars more than their monthly rent allotment. Paula explained their budget and asked the woman if she'd possibly come down in price. At first the landlady said nothing. Then she said, "I want to meet you." Knowing their chances were slim, Larry and Paula had little hope as they went to meet her.

After meeting the Dinkinses and considering their offer, the woman changed her mind and agreed to let them rent her lovely four-bedroom, two-bath house for one year at their rent allotment rate! "If we like you, maybe another year," she said. It turned out she was from one of the wealthiest Thai families in town, and they could easily manage the lower rent.

Before long, the house seemed like home, and the Dinkinses lived there for three years before returning to the States for furlough. This house actually had more space than the other one. Since it was right by the church, the pastor let Larry hold his Bible extension program there each week, and the students could walk to the house for tea afterward. The Dinkinses became good friends with the pastor and his wife and with the landlady and her husband, sharing meals together and enjoying each other's company.

When they left for the U.S., the landlady told Paula, "I'm so glad we got to know you and that you rented our home."

"What changed your mind and caused you to let us, even though we couldn't pay enough?" Paula asked.

"I felt like it was love at first sight when we saw you and your family! Hurry back to Chiang Mai!"

God had saved just the right house for the Dinkinses and had given Paula a clear picture of the adjacent church so they'd find it. He had even overcome the obstacle of the rental price, preparing the Thai woman's heart for the dramatic reduction in the monthly rent.

Sometimes we think God hasn't answered our prayers unless we receive what we want. But God answers *all* our prayers—sometimes yes, sometimes wait, and sometimes no. When God says no or answers differently than we expect, most of us grow frustrated or angry just as Paula did. But while we see life from a limited, finite viewpoint, God sees the beginning and ending of all things and everything in between. When we thank Him for closing a door, we can discover the window He wants to open for our best.

DISCUSSION OPENERS

1. We don't usually share times when God says no to our prayer requests, but sometimes God knows that no is better than yes. Can you think of a time when you received a disappointing result from your prayers, only to discover that God knew best and later brought something better or showed His glory through the situation? What did you learn from that experience?

2. Think of people in the Bible to whom God said no. (For example, Job, Jeremiah, Jesus, and Paul.) What can we learn from their experiences? From the way they responded to God in the midst of struggle?

3. How did God prepare the Dinkinses for the house *He* had picked out, and how did He open doors once they found it? What does this show us about God's care and provision?

SCRIPTURES FOR GOING DEEPER

Psalm 77; 88
Habakkuk 3:17–19
2 Corinthians 12:8–10

A PRAYER

Lord, help us to trust You when You say no.
You alone know how our prayer requests fit into Your purposes,
so help us thank You and wait for Your working and Your perfect timing.
Give us extra trust in Your plan and Your promises,
and help us remember that You have a future and a hope for us,
even when things look unclear or we feel disappointed.
So often, Lord, we want our way;
help us want Your way more!
In Jesus' name, amen.

A PARTING THOUGHT

"He is not one of those who give readiest what they prize least. He does not care to give anything but his best, or that which will prepare for it. Not many years may pass before you confess, 'You are a God who hears prayer, and gives a better answer.' You may come to see that the desire of your deepest heart would have been frustrated by having what seemed its embodiment then. That God should as a loving Father listen, hear, consider, and deal with the request after the perfect tenderness of his heart, is to me enough."

GEORGE MacDONALD

TWENTY-NINE

The Grateful Leper

≈

Give thanks in all circumstances,
for this is God's will for you in Christ Jesus.
1 THESSALONIANS 5:18

Eli knew that Jews didn't like Samaritans, so all his life he had stayed away from them. As a little boy, he didn't understand why Jews yelled at him and made fun of him. His mother had tried to explain that some people just didn't know any better, but that didn't make it *feel* any better. As Eli grew, he had tried to shrug off the insults, but they lodged deep within him just the same.

Eli had become a man and had made a life for himself, finding friends and learning a trade: weaving. But one day after hours at his loom, he stopped to stretch, absent-mindedly scratching his neck. Odd, he thought, that place has itched for a couple of weeks now. Slowly a dark thought uncoiled in the back of his mind. No. That's impossible. It couldn't really happen...not to me! Why, I've been so careful. I don't even know anyone with...He hated to say it, even in his thoughts.

His hands went cold and his mind raced. He had to see for himself. Even though it wasn't yet time to leave, Eli snuck out of the weaver's shop. He knew his neighbor had a small, burnished brass mirror. If he could just borrow it, maybe he could alleviate his fears.

Even now, years later, he could still feel the cold metal handle as he stared into the mirror. There it was: that pale, raised, rough patch of skin. Leprosy.

He had known instantly what it meant. If you had leprosy, you were truly an outcast. You had to live outside the city, your only company other lepers. No one would touch you, no one would come near you. Not even fellow Samaritans.

Eli had thought he was isolated before, but that was nothing compared to now. Leaving his family had been the hardest thing he had ever done. He had moved outside his village where a small group of lepers lived…men and women he had, until now, shunned. Now he was one of them.

During his first days in the colony, Eli had stayed to himself, withdrawn in his memories. At first he saw the others as a group of dirty bodies and mangled faces. But gradually he sorted out a few of the other men: Ben, a bitter man with a biting wit; Ananias, withdrawn and silent; Barnabas, the oldest of them all. And then there was Reuben. It was Reuben's wistful eyes that first drew Eli to him. Slowly, the two men became friends.

One day, as Eli crouched beside the village road, begging for coins, he heard Reuben's shuffle behind him. "Eli! Guess what?"

What now? Eli thought. It hadn't taken him long to realize that, with little to do but beg and watch, his new leper "family" were masters of local gossip.

"That new rabbi is coming!" Reuben's eyes flashed with excitement. "You know, the one with all the special powers that the priests hate."

"Really?" This time, it really was news. "He's coming here?"

"I heard two priests talking about it as they went by. They said he was headed this way and should be here tomorrow. They weren't happy at all. Eli, do you think it's all true?"

"About his powers? I don't know. I wish it were. But even then, he's a Jew and we're Samaritan lepers. He has two very strong reasons not to come near us."

That night the men talked it over. Could this man really heal? Or would he be a fake like all the others? Finally, Reuben had had enough.

"What do we have to lose?" he demanded. "Will people ignore us more? Laugh at us more? Stay further away from us?"

Eli had to agree with Reuben. They had nothing to lose. It was a small hope, but anything was better than dull desperation.

The next day, he, Reuben, and eight others stood along the road, watching the people coming into town. Finally they saw a small band of men walking slowly through the noonday heat and dust. Eli gulped. If they were going to draw the rabbi's attention, now was the time. Would he shun them? Would he try to heal them and fail? Or could he truly heal as they had heard?

Eli turned to Reuben. "Quick! This is our chance." Eli saw his desperation mirrored in Reuben's eyes as they turned to meet the coming band of men. "Jesus! Master! Have pity on us!"

The little band of men stopped. "Do you think he heard us?" Eli asked. "Look...he's coming toward us!"

Slowly Jesus approached the ten lepers. The dust from the road was thick in his robes and hair. He looked tired, but he regarded each of them kindly. For years no one had even looked upon them—now this rabbi was not only looking them in the eye, he was doing so in a spirit of gentleness, respect, and love. "Go. Show yourselves to the priests," he told them.

Startled, Eli's eyes met Reuben's. *Do I look as puzzled as Reuben does?* he wondered. The rabbi's expression had been kind, but there was also a hint of something else in his eyes. Was it humor? A challenge? Eli wasn't sure. But he did feel something within him that said, Do what this man says. Go to the temple.

He wanted to argue because he knew the priests would be furious when ten lepers walked into their holy temple. He didn't need to face any more rejection in his life.

But there was that thing inside him that said, Go. Do what the rabbi said. Eli realized that all the others must be feeling the same thing, for all of them had turned toward town. In fact, they began running! Eli ran, too, and as he did, he felt something so new and wonderful that he thought he must be imagining it.

He felt his feet!

His feet had been numb for years, but today he felt the sharp bite of gravel on the soles of his feet. Startled, Eli stopped in amazement. The patches of leathery skin were gone. His flesh was soft and new. His feet tingled!

And then his whole body began to grow hot with excitement. Cautiously, Eli put a hand to his neck. That long-familiar numb place was gone. His neck was smooth. He was healed!

The others had stopped as well, stunned by the pain in their formerly numb feet and hands, by the brand-new baby softness of their skin. They were well and alive! They began running even faster toward town.

Eli, however, stood rooted to the spot. He could feel his feet! He looked back and saw the rabbi still standing there in the dusty road, watching as the men ran away. This rabbi, this Jesus, had given him back his life...and he was running away! How could he run from a man like that?

Almost before Eli knew it, his happy new feet ran not toward town but back to the rabbi. As he ran, the joy in his heart bubbled up into his mouth and flowed from his lips: "Thank you, Rabbi!" he shouted. "Thank you, Elohim! Thank you for sending us this man!"

Eli didn't care what anyone thought. He just ran to Jesus and flung himself into the dust at the feet of this wonderful man. "Thank you," Eli breathed. "Thank you for giving me back my life."[1]

DISCUSSION OPENERS

1. Long ago Jesus gave us back our lives by dying on the cross and rising from the dead. Have you thanked Him recently for doing that?

2. Do you ever feel outcast? Explain. How can Jesus help you when you feel alone?

3. Spend some time thanking God for the large and small things He has done for you. Cultivate a grateful heart. You're no longer an isolated outcast; you're a child of God!

SCRIPTURES FOR GOING DEEPER

Psalm 103:1–5
Isaiah 61:1–3
Colossians 1:12

A PRAYER

God, we are grateful for everything You've given us.
Not only have You done huge and remarkable things such as
forgiving all our sins and making us Your children,
You've filled each day with new life—
birds singing at sunrise, smiles from friends,
comfort when things don't go right.
Like the leper who remembered, we always want to come back to You
and say "Thank You!"
So here we sit at Your feet in prayer,
and like the leper we breathe a prayer of thanks:
"Thank You for giving us back our lives."
In Jesus' name, amen.

A PARTING THOUGHT

"When we succeed in truly thanking God, we feel good at heart. The reason is that we have been created to give glory to God, now and forevermore. And every time we do so, we feel that we are in harmony with His plans and purposes for our lives. That is why it is so blessed."

O. HALLESBY

THIRTY

Pardon for Traitors

Be kind and compassionate to one another, forgiving each other,
just as in Christ God forgave you.

EPHESIANS 4:32

There's an old saying: "All's fair in love and war." Nothing could be further from the truth.

During the Revolutionary War, a ragtag colonial army fought a powerful British one. Often outnumbered, hungry and cold, the last thing the revolutionary warriors needed was for one of their own soldiers to turn traitor and sell secrets to the enemy. But Michael Wittman did exactly that, and quite successfully. But one day his fellow soldiers found out and captured him. They put him on trial, found him guilty of spying for the British, and sentenced him to death. He sat in jail awaiting his hanging.

The night before Wittman's scheduled execution, a visitor called on General George Washington, the leader of the Revolutionary Army. The visitor was Peter Miller, a white-haired old man who had done a great deal to benefit Washington and his troops. Washington greeted Miller warmly.

"General, I have a favor to ask of you," Miller said. "I've come to ask for the pardon of Michael Wittman."

Washington was astonished. "What? The man is a traitor. He's sold

us out to the British and done everything he can to destroy us."
Washington shook his head. "Peter, we're at war. This man deserves his
sentence, and I can't afford to be lenient, even if he is a friend of yours."

"Friend?" Miller exploded. "General, that man is no friend of mine.
He's been my enemy for years."

"Then why would you come here and ask for a man like that to be
set free?" Washington asked, puzzled.

"Because...Jesus did as much for me."

A silence fell over the room. Then Washington's steps echoed
loudly from the wood floor as he walked away. A few anxious minutes
ticked by. Then Washington's steps again resounded across the floor,
this time approaching Miller. Washington carried a piece of paper in his
hand: "A pardon for Michael Wittman." As he handed it to Peter Miller,
Washington said, "My friend, I thank you for this."[1]

Most of us will never have the chance to plead to a powerful general for a traitor's pardon during wartime. But God invites us everyday
to plead for the pardon of "traitors" we know. Because everyone has
sinned, everyone is a traitor to God and deserves the death sentence.
Yet God loved us so much that He sent His own Son, Jesus, to serve
that death sentence for us. And just like Peter Miller, our gratefulness
at the amazing pardon we've received should compel us to plead with
God for the pardon of others.

All's fair in love and war? There's nothing less fair than a traitor
going free...and nothing more loving.

DISCUSSION OPENER

1. Have you ever had someone betray you? What was the situation? What would it be like to pray for that person?

2. How did George Washington's heart change as a result of Peter
Miller's plea? What might happen within you if you pray for the traitor
in your life?

3. Pray together for the traitors you know, asking God to help those
people know the forgiveness and freedom available through Jesus
Christ.

SCRIPTURES FOR GOING DEEPER

Luke 11:4

Colossians 3:13

A PRAYER

Dear Jesus, help us understand what You did for us on the cross.
We want to realize where we would have been without You
and wake up each day knowing You've changed our lives.
As we live in that awareness,
help us see those around us as people You want to forgive and free.
Remind us that when we see a person as unforgivable,
You see someone ripe for forgiveness, from You and from me.
In Jesus' name, amen.

A PARTING THOUGHT

"When we realize that we are all sinners needing forgiveness, it will be easy for us to forgive others."

MOTHER TERESA[2]

THIRTY-ONE

Praying on the Spot

≈

Don't worry about anything; instead, pray about everything.
Tell God what you need, and thank him for all he has done.
If you do this, you will experience God's peace, which
is far more wonderful than the human mind can understand.

PHILIPPIANS 4:6–7 (NLT)

Jay is a young man with Down's syndrome, a deteriorating heart condition, and a speech disability. While these conditions limit him in some ways, they haven't inhibited the effectiveness of his prayers. Jay prays on the spot whenever something happens. Whatever the need, Jay lifts it to heaven, knowing God can help. He takes to heart Paul's admonition for us to pray about everything, not worry about anything, and with thanksgiving, let our requests be made known to God (Philippians 4:6).

One weekend, Jay's grandparents (his mother's parents) visited from out of town. Jay's grandfather suffers from Alzheimer's disease, and Granddad often becomes confused and disoriented. So the day he arrived at Jay's house, Granddad felt lost even though he had been in the house dozens of times before. He didn't know where his wife (Grandmama, as Jay calls her) was, although she sat right beside him. He couldn't find the bathroom. He began to cry and became so distraught that the family had to take him and Grandmama to a nearby hotel to calm down and spend the night. Everyone in Jay's family had looked forward to this visit; now it had fizzled, and they wondered if they'd have any enjoyable time together.

The next morning, Jay's mom Louise picked up Grandmama and Granddad from the hotel and brought them back to the house. Sitting at the table, Granddad began to look just as confused as the day before. Louise and the other adults in the family tried everything they knew to make him feel comfortable, but nothing worked. He only grew more disoriented and sad.

Suddenly Jay left his toys, walked over to Granddad, placed one hand on Granddad's shoulder, and lifted his other hand to heaven. Simply, in his own unique words, unclear perhaps to those around him but perfectly clear to God, Jay asked God to heal his grandfather and ended his prayer with, "Thank You, God. Praise You, Jesus!"

In a matter of moments, a smile came over Granddad's face as clarity returned to his mind. He knew everyone in the family and could remember the location of the bathroom and other important places and things. It was as if a thick fog had blown away and a sweet peace had replaced it.

Jay doesn't speak clearly, and when he prayed for his grandfather most of the adults didn't understand what he was saying. But God had heard every word.

DISCUSSION OPENERS

1. Do you ever feel too inadequate to pray? How might Jay's story encourage you that God hears and understands your prayers?

2. Do you ever feel tempted to discount someone else's prayers because that person has disabilities or seems too young? How might people such as this serve as valuable prayer partners?

3. Have you ever been like the adults in this story, forgetting to pray at a critical time? What happened in that situation?

4. How can you develop an attitude toward prayer like Jay had?

SCRIPTURES FOR GOING DEEPER

Matthew 7:11
1 Thessalonians 5:17
James 5:16b–18

A PRAYER

Lord, we want to be available to You whenever You call.
Please keep us tuned to Your calls for prayer.
Help us develop the inclination to pray about everything that concerns us,
for as we seek You and Your Kingdom first,
You will add "all things" to our lives.
Thank You from the bottom of our hearts!
In Jesus' name, amen.

A PARTING THOUGHT

"Sudden prayer burdens are God's SOS calls for your help. If at all possible, interrupt what you're doing and pray at once for the need God places upon you."

WESLEY DUEWELL

Pray Spontaneously

Do you want to help your children learn to pray on the spot as Jay did? Then model that kind of prayer! When your children approach you with a worry or a problem, pray about it with them. When you find yourself in a heated disagreement with your kids, stop and pray. If a speeding ambulance passes you while you're driving, pray for the people in the ambulance, for their families, and for the doctors who will care for the injured people when they arrive at the hospital. When someone you know requests prayer, don't say "I'll pray for you" and go quickly on your way; instead, stop and pray with that person right then and there.

Praying spontaneous prayers like these shows your children that God cares about every part of their lives. They, too, willl learn to pray on the spot.

THIRTY-TWO

Putting on God's Armor

Use every piece of God's armor to resist the enemy in the time of evil, so that after the battle you will still be standing firm. Stand your ground, putting on the sturdy belt of truth and the body armor of God's righteousness. For shoes, put on the peace that comes from the Good News, so that you will be fully prepared. In every battle you will need faith as your shield to stop the fiery arrows aimed at you by Satan. Put on salvation as your helmet, and take the sword of the Spirit, which is the word of God.

EPHESIANS 6:13–17 (NLT)

ang! Bang!" shouted Austin, an energetic four-year-old, as he raced in for family devotions. Some nights he bounded in wielding a new space gun, and other evenings he showed up with pockets full of action figures so he could imagine them in battle.

Austin loved guns, cowboys, and *Star Wars* action play; he did *not* love sitting still for a long time and having to be quiet. Whenever he and Mom and Dad sat down for devotions, Austin had a hard time paying attention to the Bible stories. He giggled and fidgeted during prayer time and couldn't wait until it was over so he could return to his toys.

His mom, Terri, understood that part of her son's behavior was normal for a four-year-old boy. But she also wanted Austin to know the importance of prayer and to grow in his relationship with Jesus. "God, what should I do about this?" Terri prayed. "How can I get Austin interested in prayer?"

As she continued to intercede for her son, God gave her a great idea for putting prayer in Austin's terms. Terri phoned her husband at work to share her brainstorm with him. He liked it, too, and on the way home from work he stopped by a store and found just what they needed.

That night when they sat down for family devotions, Terri explained to Austin that he was a "prayer warrior" and that God listened to every word he prayed. Then Austin's dad brought out the silver poster-board set of "spiritual armor," and they showed Austin how to dress in it.

"You can wear the helmet, Austin, because you've accepted Jesus as your Savior and Lord, so He's your commander in all the battles you face." That sounded great to Austin, and when he put on the shiny, silver Helmet of Salvation, it fit perfectly.

"Here's your sword," Terri said, handing it to him. "It stands for God's Word that we're hiding in your heart, and it's the best defense against anything our enemy Satan throws at you."

"Look at this shield! Wow! It's so big!" Austin exclaimed, holding it in front of him just as he had seen soldiers do in movies.

"That's your Shield of Faith. As you trust in God and put all your faith in Him, you'll be protected and secure in life," his dad instructed.

Over the next few days, Austin's parents explained the other pieces of spiritual armor. And somehow the message must have reached Austin because two months later in Sunday school, when Austin's teacher asked if anyone wanted to pray, Austin stood right up and said, "I will pray...*I'm a prayer warrior!*" As Austin fervently prayed for two classmates who were sick and another who was being bullied at school, his teacher began to cry. "Austin, God loves to hear your prayers!" she said.

As Austin understood more and more that his prayers could make a difference, prayer became an important part of his family's daily life together. Now they pray about everything: meals, car accidents they see, storms, and struggles. And while Austin still asks God if his favorite Scooby Doo pillow can go to heaven and for God to provide toys he *really* wants, his prayers are changing and becoming more evangelistic. He prays for "bad guys" to come to know Jesus. He prays for friends and family and a missionary he calls "Mission Papa." Now instead of finding prayer boring, he finds it important. He's in Jesus' army and has the armor to prove it!

Whether we're four years old or forty, we're *all* prayer warriors. And we're in a very real war. In fact, God tells us we're soldiers in His army (see Psalm 110:2–3 and 2 Timothy 2:3–4). And in a sense, all prayer is spiritual warfare because we're entering enemy territory (planet Earth) and petitioning the Lord to bring His kingdom to it.

God wouldn't send us into the fray without protection and equipment. He has provided us everything we need to stand firm against the enemy and withstand all the trials and difficulties we encounter. Each piece of armor described in Ephesians 6 represents Christ's provision for us to help us fight spiritual battles:

- The *Belt of Truth* reminds us of the truth that God loves us and that nothing in our lives is outside His care and concern. We are His children and nothing can separate us from His love.
- Jesus is the "author and perfecter of our faith" (Hebrews 12:2), and that's why He can provide us with a *Shield of Faith* to deflect the discouragement or fear the enemy tries to foist on us.
- Isaiah 61:10 says we are clothed in His righteousness; putting on the *Breastplate of Righteousness* reminds us that we're in right standing with God only because of Jesus' sacrifice on the cross.
- So often the enemy tries to drop wrong thoughts or fears into our minds and hearts, but the *Helmet of Salvation* protects us and assures us that our salvation and our security—both here and for all eternity—are in Christ.
- Since Jesus is the Living Word, keeping our minds full of Scripture, the *Sword of the Spirit* guards us from Satan's deceptions and lies.
- Jesus is also our peace (Ephesians 2:14), and when we fit our feet with the *Gospel of Peace,* peace will fill us and follow us everywhere we go.

So put on the armor, wear it every day, and go for it! Listen for God's voice and embark on the adventures He sets before you, whether praying for those in need or reaching out to friends with the gospel. With your armor on, you're ready to fight the enemy and win!

DISCUSSION OPENERS

1. What spiritual battles do you face on a regular basis? This week in particular? Who's your enemy?

2. Why should you "put on the armor of God"?

3. How can each piece of spiritual armor help you combat the enemy? What happens when you forget to wear each piece of armor? (If your family wants to be creative, set out some cardboard, markers, scissors, glue, tape, and any other craft materials you can use to create your own set of spiritual armor. Use the items as visual aids during your discussion. Place the items somewhere prominent in your home to remind everyone to put on their spiritual armor every day.)

SCRIPTURES FOR GOING DEEPER

Psalm 91
2 Corinthians 10:3–5
1 Peter 5:6–9

A PRAYER

Lord, we thank You for all You've provided for us in Christ Jesus,
and we want to wear Your spiritual armor today!
So by faith we don the Belt of Truth,
remembering the truth that we are Yours and nothing can come between
You and us.
We put on the Breastplate of Righteousness,
the righteousness we have only because of Your grace.
We put on the shoes of the Gospel of Peace.
Keep our hearts peaceful so we can spread peace wherever we go.
Help us use the Sword of the Spirit, Your Word,
and the Shield of Faith to fend off the enemy's fiery darts.
Guard our thoughts with Your Helmet of Salvation,

and help us stand firm, pray with all our might, and trust You for victory!
In Jesus' name, amen.

A PARTING THOUGHT

"All prayer is spiritual warfare. Every prayer that gains ground for God's kingdom loses ground for the enemy. To pray is to be locked in battle with spiritual forces. Spiritual warfare is not a single type of praying. Prayer is warfare."

—JENNIFER DEAN[1]

Providing Prayer Cover

Children today, even young ones, face spiritual battles. The enemy doesn't play fair, waiting until they're older to attack them, so we can't wait to provide "prayer cover" for them. Just as air force jets provide air cover for an impending military maneuver, we parents can cover our children in spiritual and physical protection by interceding for them daily. Pray that your children will hide God's Word in their hearts so they won't sin against Him (Psalm 119:11); that they'll come to know Christ at an early age (2 Timothy 1:5); that the Holy Spirit will fill them with knowledge of God's will; that God will show them the mighty ways He'll work when they pray; that they'll realize their vital role in God's plan today. As you pray, God will prepare them for the battles they face today and every day.

THIRTY-THREE

What Should I Pray?

*The rain and snow come down from the heavens and
stay on the ground to water the earth.
They cause the grain to grow, producing seed for the farmer and
bread for the hungry. It is the same with my word.
I send it out, and it always produces fruit. It will accomplish all I want it to,
and it will prosper everywhere I send it.*

ISAIAH 55:10–11 (NLT)

Heather slumped in her chair as the middle school orchestra began tuning up. *I want out of this class so badly…I just want to quit,* she thought. *I'm tired of Mrs. Sargeant. She's always saying mean things to me.*

Heather's friend Jenny, also fed up with the class, had quit the day before. Now Heather had no one to talk to. Seventh grade had been depressing enough; she didn't need this class to dread every day.

Heather had tried so hard to move up in the orchestra, but progress had eluded her. *I'm almost last chair,* she continued lamenting. *And I'll never move up, no matter how hard I try or how good I play—Mrs. Sargeant doesn't even notice. What's the use?*

On this particular day, each student had to play a selected piece for the teacher. As Heather played, she could see the first and second violin students giving her a look that said, "Oh, she's off-key again. No wonder our orchestra is so bad!" Their disdain only made her more nervous, and she missed a few notes. Then, when the first and second violin students played, Mrs. Sargeant gushed about how fabulous they sounded. Heather tried to tune out the teacher's comments, but jealousy overcame her, and she almost ran from the room.

When the bell rang, Heather headed for the bus—alone. She got off at her stop, stormed into her house, threw her books and violin case on the floor, and told her mom, "That's it. Jenny quit orchestra, and so am I!"

"Not so fast, Heather," her mother, Melanie, replied. "You've been taking lessons for two years, and think of all the work you've put into practice. I think you'll regret it if you quit now."

"But, Mom, it's awful, and Mrs. Sargeant hates me! I just want to drop out."

"Instead of dropping out, why don't you keep playing and pray about it?"

"But I don't know what to pray," Heather moaned, "except, 'Hey, God, could you get me out of this class?'"

Melanie pulled two sodas from the refrigerator and sat at the kitchen counter with her daughter. "God's Word can be a light to your path, and His promises can direct your prayers. And His Word doesn't return empty without accomplishing something. If you ask Him, you could find out what His Word says. It could make a big difference."

Heather reluctantly agreed to give it a try. Later that evening, as she sat at her desk flipping through her Bible, two verses popped out at her. The first was Psalm 5:12: "For surely, O LORD, you bless the righteous; you surround them with your favor as with a shield." The second verse was Philippians 4:13: "I can do everything through him who gives me strength."

Everything? Even violin? Heather wondered. She wasn't sure, but she thought it sounded encouraging. *A shield? I could use one of those to protect me from the verbal barbs Mrs. Sargeant throws at me.*

Heather repeated the verses again, then prayed them to God as she described her circumstances. "God, I'm really discouraged about violin. I need Your help. I don't feel like I'm a very good violin player, but You said I can do *everything* through You because You'll give me strength.

So I'm going to take You at Your Word! Give me the strength I need to keep practicing and get better. Please surround me with Your favor just like a shield, especially when I'm in orchestra. And help my relationship with my teacher."

Things didn't improve overnight, but Heather continued playing and praying. She practiced violin two to three hours a day and kept asking God for favor with her music teacher and for strength to do her best—just as the verses said.

As time went on, Heather didn't dread orchestra class quite as much. Sometimes she even felt twinges of joy as she drew her bow across the strings and listened to the sound all the instruments made together. When she felt discouraged, she prayed for favor and strength and thanked God for His promised help.

About nine months later, in the spring semester of her eighth-grade year, Heather again sat in orchestra class, but this time she sat in a different place. She had just moved up to second chair, one chair away from first violin! As she picked up her violin, her mind flashed back to that day in seventh grade when she wanted to quit. She realized how far she had come, moving from last chair to almost the top of the string section. "Thank You, God!" she prayed. "Being part of the orchestra is more fun than I thought...and Mrs. 'S' isn't so bad after all."

Her thoughts were interrupted when Mrs. Sargeant tapped her baton on the music stand to direct their current piece, *Light Cavalry Overture* by Von Suppe. Suddenly, the teacher looked up and smiled at Heather while she spoke to the rest of the class. "If I were giving an award for the most improved student," Mrs. Sargeant said, "it would go to Heather!"

Have you ever, like Heather, not known what to pray? Ever wondered about God's will in a given situation? The more we read His Word, allowing His words to abide in us and guide our prayers, the more we pray according to God's will and plan instead of our own. On many issues, God doesn't leave us to guess what His will is. He clearly reveals it through the pages of His Book.

As Heather talked with her mom and searched through Scripture, God seemed to tell her to persevere not only with practicing violin but with praying. As she did both, He began to work, blessing Heather more than she had asked or imagined. Praying God's Word isn't a magic formula guaranteeing us whatever we want, but we can't go wrong as we study it and incorporate it into our conversations with Him. His promises and words have power, and when we pray them, we know our prayers are right on target.

DISCUSSION OPENERS

1. How did praying God's Word affect Heather's situation? What changed as a result of her prayers?

2. God promises us special effectiveness when we pray in accordance with His will (see 1 John 5:14–15). Do you face a situation in which you don't know His will? Ask Him to show you a verse or passage of Scripture that applies to your situation, and let His Word guide your prayers.

SCRIPTURES FOR GOING DEEPER

Jeremiah 15:16
Matthew 4:4
Romans 10:17
1 John 5:14–15

A PRAYER

Father God, thank You for the awesome promises in Your Word,
our perfect prayer manual.
Thank You that as we pray, Your word encourages us
and accomplishes what You've planned.
Open our eyes to specific verses that can shape our petitions
so You can receive the glory.
In Jesus' name, amen.

A PARTING THOUGHT

"God's promises are given...to show the direction in which we may ask and the extent to which we may expect an answer. Though the Bible be crowded with golden promises, yet they will be inoperative until we turn them into prayer."

F. B. MEYER

Praying the Word

As kids read God's Word, they encounter powerful ways to pray. When they read that He is their Rock, Shield, Victor, Sovereign Lord, and Promise Keeper, encourage them to praise Him for those characteristics. When your children bring a verse such as Isaiah 11:2 home on a Sunday school project, incorporate that verse into your family prayers: "Lord, may Your Spirit rest upon Ashley and Justin today at school—the Spirit of wisdom and understanding, the Spirit of counsel and of power; the Spirit of knowledge and of the fear of the Lord." Then encourage your children to pray that verse, too, and trust God to fulfill it.

THIRTY-FOUR

God Hears Us

Where can I go from Your Spirit? Or where can I flee from Your presence?
If I ascend to heaven, You are there; If I make my bed in Sheol, behold,
You are there.... If I dwell in the remotest part of the sea,
Even there Your hand will lead me, and Your right hand will lay hold of me.
PSALM 139:7–10 (NASB)

Irina was a brown-haired, ten-year-old girl growing up in Odessa, a bleak city in the Soviet Union, during Nikita Khrushcher's rule. Like other children her age, she spent her school days enduring hours of boring lectures and indoctrination into Communist thinking. Every day she heard, "God doesn't exist. He's just a fairy tale that people have made up." Irina wondered why the teachers kept talking about a fake God. She began to wonder whether He was actually real, that maybe her teachers were so afraid of Him that they didn't want children to believe in Him.

One day she was sitting in class, thinking what it would be like if God were real, when it started to snow—a rare occurrence in Odessa. Oh, how she wanted to go out and throw snowballs with her friends, but she knew the snow would melt long before the school day would end. Just then, Irina uttered her first prayer, something like this: "God, if You really exist and are so powerful, make it keep snowing."

The snow kept falling and falling. In fact, the snowflakes became so big and fell so heavily that Odessa experienced its biggest snowfall in sixty years. Not only that, school was canceled and Irina's wish came true: She got to go outside and play in the snow!

After that first answered prayer, Irina began to talk to God secretly when she was alone in bed. Though she still had to endure years of atheistic schooling and had no access to a Bible or to anyone who could tell her about Jesus, Irina sought to know God. In her nighttime prayers, she asked God many questions.

One of those nights while Irina was talking to God, a small voice within her seemed to say, "Don't worry, you will find out what you need to know when the time comes." On another night, she wrote a poem expressing her desire to find God. As she wrote, she felt a warm, loving presence. She knew then that God hadn't abandoned her, that He didn't mind that she didn't really know how to pray. He was with her—she wasn't alone!

Several years passed. When Irina was twenty-three, someone gave her a Bible so she could read God's words for herself. As she read, she knew she was a Christian and that God truly loved her and had been leading her all her life.

At age twenty-eight, Irina, because of her Christian faith and witness, was sentenced to seven years' hard labor and seven more years of internal exile (banished to a bleak place within her own country). But in spite of all the terrible things done to her, she survived and was eventually released. She later wrote a book expressing her gratitude for the many Christians around the world who had prayed for her while she was in prison. In that book, she described how she had experienced God's presence over and over because of other people's prayers. His presence came much as she had experienced it as a child: God's loving eye watching over her, the sense of incredible warmth in a freezing cold prison cell. Through her horrible ordeal, God continually assured Irina of His love.[1]

The prayers of a ten-year-old girl who had no idea whether God existed...the prayers of people across the world for one persecuted Christian...God heard them all. What will He hear from you today?

DISCUSSION OPENERS

1. Irina's story shows us that God hears us and loves us even when we don't know much about Him. What does this tell you about how God loves you and desires a relationship with you?

2. What happened as people around the world prayed for Irina?

3. What would you like to know about God today? Ask Him to reveal Himself to you.

4. Who do you know who needs to experience God's presence in a special way today? Pray for that person.

SCRIPTURES FOR GOING DEEPER

John 10:28–30
John 16:33
Romans 8:37
James 1:2–4

A PRAYER

Lord, thank You that You hear us,
and that no matter where we are—
even in bleak, cold lands across the world or in prison—
nothing can keep out Your warmth and comfort,
no bars can close out Your love,
and no obstacles can block our prayers.
Hallelujah!
In Jesus' name, amen.

A PARTING THOUGHT

"More things are wrought by prayer than this world dreams of."
ALFRED, LORD TENNYSON

THIRTY-FIVE

When You're Afraid

≈

For God has not given us a spirit of fear and
timidity, but of power, love, and self-discipline.
2 TIMOTHY 1:7 (NLT)

"I don't have to go to kindergarten, do I, Mom?" five-year-old Greg asked after he'd heard the neighborhood kids talking about school. The first day of school was months away, but every time Greg heard anything about it, he became apprehensive. And even though the school building stood right across the street from his house, the thought of kindergarten terrified him.

This wasn't a great surprise. Greg had trouble with any kind of change, always clinging to his mom in uncertain times. But during the next few weeks, his anxiety increased with every mention of kindergarten until his parents realized they couldn't mention the *k* word without Greg becoming hysterical.

At wit's end, Stephanie held her son in her arms and rocked him while she silently asked God for help.

"Do you believe God can help you?" she finally asked Greg.

"Well, yes, Mom. But could we ask Him right now?"

"Dear God," Stephanie prayed, "Greg's five now and going through changes. He's going to start kindergarten soon and is very afraid. Please let Greg's angel put a hand on his shoulder as he walks into school, and let him know You're there with him. Give him strength, and let *something* happen that will make him feel better about school. In Jesus' name, amen."

When Greg's dad, Carl, learned about his son's fears, he began praying, too. At bedtime he prayed individually with Greg, and at other times, the whole family—Mom, Dad, Greg, and his two-year-old sister, Audrey—interceded for him.

Day after day during the summer, these prayers temporarily calmed Greg. Finally the first day of school arrived. That morning Greg silently, reluctantly, and tearfully got dressed. Mom took his photo as he glumly stood in the doorway, backpack in hand. Then they held hands and walked across the street to the school. Upon arrival at the kindergarten classroom, most of the kids said happy good-byes to their parents, but not Greg. He and another child wailed.

"Why don't you walk around the halls to let Greg get familiar with the school?" the teacher suggested. So mother and son walked to the water fountain, took a drink, and looked at the playground.

Suddenly, a voice called, "Hi, Greg!"

They turned around and were surprised to see "Miss Lisa," Greg's favorite swimming instructor from the local YMCA. Relief rushed over the kindergartner's face. Someone he knew and loved! Miss Lisa's warm smile calmed him immediately, and she explained that she worked at the school.

After their chat, Miss Lisa gave Greg a hug. He turned and walked confidently into his classroom. With a hug and a kiss for his mom, Greg said a cheerful, "Bye! See ya later!"

"Mom," Greg observed that night, "God sent Miss Lisa to be the angel we prayed for, didn't He? He knew just what I needed!"

Seeing how God took care of his fears, Greg started praying about everything. Now at the "grown-up" age of eight, Greg initiates praying for his younger sister, who has spina bifida.

Like Greg, lots of kids fear things: the dark, the unknown, imaginary bogeymen in their closets, lightning, and thunderstorms. Maybe you have something you fear. Whatever makes you afraid, you can pray about it. God cares about the things that worry and scare you. And when you realize He wants to take care of you, you'll probably feel encouraged to bring even more of your concerns to Him.

Remember, nothing is too big or frightening for God to handle. Not even kindergarten!

DISCUSSION OPENERS

1. Are you afraid of anything? If so, why not bring it to God right now?

2. Do you really think God has the ability to solve your problems and deliver the help you need, even in big storms and in things beyond your control? Explain. Has He ever done that in the past? If so, how does that affect your confidence in His ability to handle your current problems?

3. Look at God's promise in Hebrews 13:5b–6. What reason does this passage give us not to fear?

4. What do you think will happen to your faith when God takes care of the things that scare or worry you?

SCRIPTURES FOR GOING DEEPER

Psalm 34:4
Psalm 56:3
Isaiah 41:13

A PRAYER

Lord, thank You that You're my Refuge and my Hiding Place.
When I'm afraid, help me trust You.
Bring Your Word to my mind in scary situations
and worrisome circumstances so I can remember
that You're my Helper and that I'm never alone.
In Jesus' name, amen.

A PARTING THOUGHT

"Be assured, if you walk with Him and look to Him and expect help from Him, He will never fail you."

GEORGE MUELLER

Helping Your Child Combat Fear

One of the best ways to help your children overcome fear is to fortify them with God's Word. More than 366 times in Scripture God tells us not to fear, and we can use those Scriptures as reminders to trust God in our scary circumstances. (Some references are provided under Scriptures for Going Deeper; others are listed at the end of this section.) To help your children learn and use these Scriptures, find specific verses that will be meaningful to them. Write the verses on three-by-five cards, one verse per card. Together with your children, memorize the verses and then pray them back to God whenever you encounter an anxious or frightening situation.

- Joshua 1:9
- 1 Chronicles 22:13
- Psalm 27:1
- Psalm 32:7
- Psalm 46:1
- Psalm 91:1–3
- Psalm 121:7–8
- Joel 2:21
- 1 John 4:18–19

THIRTY-SIX

Listening to God

Part One

*"As the heavens are higher than the earth, so are my ways higher than
your ways and my thoughts than your thoughts."*
ISAIAH 55:9

As far as Ananias knew, it was an ordinary Thursday. He had managed to wake up on time and, after a light breakfast and morning prayers, had gone to work in his shop. He was glad he had had time for prayers that morning because his day always went better when he spent time talking with God before jumping into his activities.

Ananias had grown up as a Jew, but recently he had heard the remarkable news of Jesus' resurrection from the dead. Immediately, the news captured Ananias's heart and he believed. He became a follower of Jesus—a disciple.

On this particular Thursday morning, few customers came to Ananias's shop, giving him plenty of time to think. Usually he enjoyed that, but today he couldn't help feeling worried. Just Monday morning, his friend Judas had burst into the shop and exclaimed, "Ananias, have you heard? Saul is coming here next!"

Ananias knew what that meant. Saul was a fanatical priest from Jerusalem who hated Jesus' disciples. He had made it his mission to do whatever it took to stop this "dangerous" new faith in Jesus from spreading. When Saul came to town, he went from house to house until he had found every man and woman who believed in Jesus and dragged them off to prison.

And now, this man was coming here. Ananias wondered how long it would be before he heard that knock on his door, how long before Saul took him and his wife away.

A voice interrupted his thoughts. "Ananias!"

Startled, Ananias looked up. No one had entered the shop. Was he imagining things?

Then again he heard, "Ananias!" This time, he knew that voice; it belonged to God.

"Yes, Lord," he answered.

"Go to the house of Judas on Straight Street and ask for a man from Tarsus named Saul," God said. "He is praying. In a vision, he has seen a man named Ananias come and place his hands on him to restore his sight."

Ananias was stunned. Willingly seek out this vicious persecutor? Surely not! "Lord," he protested, "I have heard many reports about this man and all the harm he has done to Your saints in Jerusalem. And he has come here with authority from the chief priests to arrest all who call on Your name."

But the Lord answered, "Go! This man is my chosen instrument to carry My name before the Gentiles and their kings and before the people of Israel. I will show him how much he must suffer for My name."

Ananias was puzzled. It didn't make any sense at all. Would God really choose a man like Saul? He said He would. And if God wanted Ananias to do something to help, he'd do it. So, wondering at himself—and at God—Ananias carefully closed his shop and set off for Straight Street.

Today, we all know the rest of the story. Saul had had his own dramatic encounter with God. God changed Saul's name to Paul, and Paul became one of God's mighty apostles. Ananias didn't know that Saul's life would change like this. For all he knew, he could have walked straight into the persecution he had feared. But Ananias knew his God, and when God spoke, he listened and obeyed.[1]

We often talk of prayer as conversation with God, and Ananias definitely had a dialog with his Lord. That dialog included listening to God. Just as we take our turn listening during our conversations with others, we need to take our turn listening to God when we pray. While we may not hear direct commands from God as Ananias did, God often does want to tell us things. Many times as we pray, we'll sense Him speaking to us through the Holy Spirit. As we tune into God's voice and do what He tells us, we will, like Ananias, experience the joy of participating in the new and wonderful things God will do.

DISCUSSION OPENERS

1. Have you ever picked up the telephone and recognized someone's voice before that person told you his or her name? If so, how did you come to recognize that person's voice?

2. How do we learn to recognize God's voice?

3. In what ways does God speak to us today?

4. Has God ever spoken to you before? If so, what did He say to you? How did you respond? What eventually happened in that situation?

SCRIPTURES FOR GOING DEEPER

Psalm 46:10
John 10:3–5, 14–16

A PRAYER

Dear God, we want to recognize when You're speaking to us.
Tune our hearts into the sound of Your voice.
And when what You say is different from what seems right to us,
give us humble hearts not just to listen to You but
to do what You say as well.
We make ourselves available for Your use,
knowing that the center of Your will is also the center of our happiness.
In Jesus' name, amen.

A PARTING THOUGHT

"A man prayed, and at first he thought that prayer was talking. But he became more and more quiet until in the end he realized that prayer is listening."

SÖREN KIERKEGAARD[2]

THIRTY-SEVEN

Listening to God

Part Two

"The sheep that are My own hear and are listening to My voice,
and I know them and they follow Me."

JOHN 10:27 (AMP)

Nine-year-old Jessica loves to try new things. Recently, she decided she wanted to play the violin. Jessica's mom and dad have always tried to encourage her interests, letting her sample all the things that capture her attention. But when Jessica expressed her desire to play violin, her mom, Sarah, knew they just couldn't afford to buy a violin if Jessica wasn't going to stick with it.

"Please, Mom?" Jessica pleaded over and over. "I know I'll love it. Puh-leeeese? Can't we get one?"

"Honey, we just can't afford it," Sarah would regretfully reply, even though part of her, too, wanted Jessica to have this chance.

One day, Sarah felt a nudge from God to let Him handle Jessica's request. "I'll tell you what," she offered her daughter. "Why don't you go and talk to God about the violin? Ask Him what He would like you to do." Jessica thought it over and decided to give it a try.

Later, Jessica returned to her mom and said, "Guess what? I was in my room and heard violin music in my heart! Mom, I think God is saying it's okay to play the violin!"

Sarah was delighted to hear that Jessica had sought God's will. But they still couldn't afford the violin. Now what should she do? "Well," she told Jessica, "why don't you ask God how He wants that to happen?"

So Jessica prayed again and returned to Sarah. "Mom, I think God wants me to use my money to help buy the violin."

Does Jessica have her violin? We don't know yet because she's still living in the middle of her story, just as all of us are. But we do know that now, each time Jessica wants to buy something, she remembers what she heard from God and asks herself, "What do I want to do with my money?" Only time will tell if she will play violin; she continues to save her money and live in faith that she will play violin someday.

Often, like Jessica, we tell God what we want. Because He's a good father, He invites us to do just that. But, also like Jessica, we need to be quiet and listen for God's answers instead of making demands of God and then going our merry way. Often, in our stillness, God gives answers that delight us, call us to new action, or simply touch our hearts in ways that bring unexpected life and love.

DISCUSSION OPENERS

1. What does it mean to listen to God? How do we know when we're really hearing God and not just our own thoughts?

2. What unique ways might God speak to you?

3. Do you have a situation in which you need to hear from God? If so, what is it? Why not take time as a family to silently listen to God right now?

SCRIPTURES FOR GOING DEEPER

Matthew 6:6
James 1:22–25

A PRAYER

Father, thank You that You invite us to come to You
with all the things that concern us.
We're glad that we can trust You
to know the right thing to do and to give us

the grace and strength we need to do it.
But we don't just want to come to You and ask.
Help us listen to You as well.
We want to be Your sheep who know Your voice and respond to it.
And when You tell us to do things we might not want to do at first,
help us know that You only ask the most loving things of and for us.
We want to love Your voice and follow it…wherever it leads.
In Jesus' name, amen.

A PARTING THOUGHT

"Jesus' life was a life of obedience. He was always listening to the Father, always attentive to his voice, always alert for his directions. Jesus was 'all ear.' That is true prayer: being all ear for God."

HENRI NOUWEN[1]

THIRTY-EIGHT

When the Lord Says Pray!

*Because you have made the LORD your refuge, and
the Most High your dwelling place, there shall no evil befall you,
nor any plague or calamity come near your tent.
For He will give His angels special charge over you to accompany and
defend and preserve you in all your ways of obedience and service.*

PSALM 91:9–11 (AMP)

The missionary rose from his campsite where he had spent the night enroute to a city for medical supplies. He extinguished his small campfire, pulled on his canvas backpack, and hopped on his bicycle to continue his ride through the African jungle. Every two weeks he made this two-day journey to collect money from a bank and purchase medicine and supplies for the small field hospital where he served. When he completed those errands, he hopped on his bike again for the two-day return trip.

When the missionary arrived in the city, he collected his money and medical supplies and was just about to leave for home when he saw two men fighting in the street. Since one of the fighters was seriously injured, the missionary stopped, treated him for his injuries, and shared the love of Christ with him. Then the missionary began his two-day trek home, stopping in the jungle again to camp overnight.

Two weeks later, as was his custom, the missionary again made the journey to the city. As he ran his various errands, a young man approached him—the same man the missionary had ministered to during his previous trip. "I knew you carried money and medicine with you," the man said, "so my friends and I followed you to your campsite in the jungle after you helped me in the street. We planned to kill you and take all the money and drugs. But just as we were about to move in and attack you, we saw twenty-six armed guards surround and protect you."

"You must be mistaken," said the missionary. "I was all alone when I spent the night in the jungle. There were no guards or anyone else with me."

"But sir, I wasn't the only one who saw the guards. My five companions saw them, too. We counted them! There were twenty-six bodyguards, too many for us to handle. Their presence stopped us from killing you."

Months later, the missionary related this story to the congregation gathered at his home church in Michigan. As he spoke, one of the men listening stood up and interrupted him, wanting to know the exact day the incident in the jungle had occurred. When the missionary identified the specific month and day of the week, the man told him "the rest of the story."

"On the exact night of your incident in Africa, it was morning here in Michigan, and I was on the golf course. I was about to putt when I felt a strong urge to pray for you. The urge was so strong, I left the golf course and called some men of our church right here in this sanctuary to join me in praying for you. Would all you men who prayed with me that day stand up?"

One by one the missionary counted the men. There were *twenty-six* of them, the exact number of "armed guards" the thwarted attackers had seen guarding him![1]

DISCUSSION OPENERS

1. What do you think might have happened if the golfer had ignored the Spirit's promptings to pray for the missionary that day?

2. Has God ever prompted you to pray for someone? Have you ever found out what happened in that person's life because of your prayers? If so, share your experience.

3. How can you become more sensitive to the Spirit's leading toward prayer? What kind of attitude do you need to foster to drop what you're doing and pray when the Lord says pray?

SCRIPTURES FOR GOING DEEPER

Mark 1:35
Ephesians 1:17
Colossians 1:9–10

A PRAYER

Lord, we want to be so responsive to Your voice
that when You say, "Pray!" we quickly fall to our knees and respond.
So we submit our plans and schedules to You,
and we invite You to interrupt us when the need arises,
whenever You have a mission to be accomplished in prayer or action.
Keep us tuned in to Your voice.
Give us hearts of obedience as Samuel had when he called,
"Speak, Lord, for your servant is listening."[2]
In Jesus' name, amen.

A PARTING THOUGHT

"When God tells us to do something, as long as it's within the limits set by Scripture, we don't have to understand it. All we need to do is obey and trust God to use our obedience to accomplish His will."

BILL HYBELS

How Can You Pray for a Missionary?

Missionaries often face near-impossible tasks with inadequate resources. They need our prayers to sustain them, but often we don't know how to pray. If you feel God has prompted you to pray for a missionary but you don't know what to pray, consider interceding for the following concerns:

- The missionary's relationship with God—pray for his or her life in God's Word and in prayer
- Emotional and physical health—pray for safe travel, good health, and emotional strength (missionaries often face situations that can cause discouragement, fear, or depression)
- Family—pray for the missionary's marriage, his or her relationships with children, and his or her relationships with extended family
- Language study and communication skills—pray for the missionary to learn the native language quickly and to become adept at sharing the Good News effectively with the people he or she encounters
- The nation or people group to whom the missionary ministers—pray that God would open the eyes of their understanding to the true knowledge of God in Christ (Ephesians 1:17–18) and for revival and renewal in the nation[3]

THIRTY-NINE

God Cares about the Little Things

Ask, and it will be given to you; seek, and you will find;
knock, and it will be opened to you.

MATTHEW 7:7 (NASB)

At a recent dental checkup, the dentist told nine-year-old Faith that she had a cavity he would need to fill. Faith's mother set the appointment for the following day.

At bedtime that night, Faith's dad listened to her stories about the X rays and how the dentist found the cavity. "What's it like to have a tooth filled, Dad?" she asked, eyes wide with curiosity.

He answered with a factual account of how the dentist would give her shots in her gums to numb her mouth, how he'd clean out the cavity with his drill, and how he'd fill up the hole with silver material. This sounded pretty scary to Faith, especially the part about the needles, and she asked, "Dad, can we pray that I'll have no more cavities?"

"Sure we can, but we can also pray that God will strengthen your tooth so you won't have any more problems." After Faith and her father prayed together, she enthusiastically said, "Thank You, God, for healing my tooth!"

"Now Faith," Dad cautioned, "sometimes when we pray for healing it happens immediately, and sometimes God chooses to work through a doctor or dentist and it takes time. You may not have enough time for healing before your appointment tomorrow. So I'm going to ask God to give you peace for your filling tomorrow…and that He'll bring health and wholeness to all your teeth. But don't get your hopes up too much. The dentist will do a good job of filling your cavity."

Despite her dad's caution, Faith was confident God would help her, and she kept praying. The next day, before giving Faith a shot of Novocain, the dentist checked her tooth again to see the exact size of the cavity. He said, "My goodness! There's no need to fill your tooth, Faith, because there's no cavity!" Faith skipped out of the dentist's office with glee and couldn't wait to share with her dad what had happened.

A week later, Faith and her family attended the Thanksgiving service at her church. The pastor invited people to share with the congregation things God had done for them. Faith stood in front of hundreds of people and told them how God had healed her tooth. Through her sharing, she reminded a large congregation of adults that we don't have to pray just about "big" things such as cancer or heart attacks; God wants to touch the many "little" things in our lives that we don't even think to share with Him.

DISCUSSION OPENERS

1. Faith asked God for something that seemed small to others but was important to her, and God answered her prayer. Would you like to ask something "small" of God? If so, what is it? Why not pray about it right now?

2. Faith asked God once to heal her cavity, and He did it. But sometimes when we want God to do something, we have to ask Him many times. In Matthew 7:7, "ask," "seek," and "knock" actually mean "ask and keep on asking," "seek and keep on seeking," and "knock and keep on knocking." Have you asked God for something, and not hearing an answer, given up? If so, why not ask Him again?

3. An important part of prayer is thanking God for His help. How did Faith express her gratitude?

4. What has God done for you in the past few weeks? How can you express your gratitude?

SCRIPTURES FOR GOING DEEPER

Psalm 34:10
Matthew 6:25–26

A PRAYER

Thank You, Lord, that You care
about everything that concerns us,
from cavities in our teeth
to hurts in our hearts.
When You do heal or intervene,
give us grateful hearts to notice and proclaim Your hand
that touches all the little things in our lives.
In Jesus' name, amen.

A PARTING THOUGHT

"Prayer is simple, as simple as a child making known its wants to its parents."

OSWALD CHAMBERS

FORTY

Prayer Lessons from a Child

At that very time [Jesus] rejoiced greatly in the Holy Spirit, and said,
"I praise You, O Father, Lord of heaven and earth, that You have hidden
these things from the wise and intelligent and have revealed them to infants."
LUKE 10:21 (NASB)

When Jesus did the impossible and raised Lazarus from the dead, He taught an important truth: "I am the resurrection and the life. He who believes in me will live, even though he dies" (John 11:25).

That truth didn't apply only to Bible times. God still does the impossible, and when He did it one day through a little boy's prayer, a whole family received multiple blessings and discovered something about God's power.

Over a ten-year span, the health of Jeffrey's grandfather had slowly deteriorated due to irreversible heart disease. Eventually he landed in the intensive care unit (ICU) with gangrene spreading through his leg because oxygen couldn't reach the limb. The doctors consulted the family about amputation but didn't recommend the surgery; Grandpa just wasn't strong enough to survive the operation. So the family decided against the surgery, opting to make him as comfortable as they could and wait for the inevitable.

Through it all, Grandpa talked and shared his testimony to whoever would listen, saying he was ready to go "when it's God's time."

On the third day after the family decided against the amputation, it looked like Grandpa's time had come. His wife, sons and daughters, and older grandchildren streamed in and out of his room, comforting him and saying good-bye. But Jeffrey's mom, Melissa, thought the sight of Grandpa so sick, with tubes coming out of him and monitors and alarms beeping, would scare Jeffrey, so she didn't take him to visit Grandpa.

That night, nine-year-old Jeffrey told his mom he wanted to go to the ICU to see his grandfather. Melissa tried to discouraged it. "But, Mom, I've got to go," the boy pleaded. "I need to see Grandpa. It seems like God wants me to be there."

So Melissa grabbed her car keys and drove Jeffrey to the hospital. After a short visit, Jeffrey held hands with his grandfather and earnestly prayed for him. Then he went into the hall and talked to the nurse, asking her about Grandpa's condition. The nurse took Jeffrey into the room and quietly explained what each tube and monitor did for Grandpa. "He's in critical condition, and the Lord will take him when He's ready," she said, after walking the young boy into the hall again.

"But I prayed for my Grandpa, and God's going to answer my prayer," Jeffrey said confidently.

After Jeffrey and his mother returned home, the boy announced, "Grandpa isn't going to die today; God told me!" He continued to intercede throughout the night.

At two o'clock the next afternoon, the phone call came. "He's gone," Melissa's brother said from the hospital room. "They've taken him off life support and shut down the monitors. All the tubes are out. They've pronounced him dead."

But just as Melissa was hanging up the phone, she heard her brother yell, "Oh my gosh...he's sitting up!" All of a sudden, Grandpa had gasped and come to life, utterly confounding the doctors and family members standing by his bed. He then sat up, clear-eyed and lucid, and started talking. "The Lord hasn't come for me yet!" he said.

Grandpa told each one of his family members how much he loved them, and then—without oxygen or medication, monitors or tubes— lived for three more days. (The doctors had given him only fifteen minutes to survive without life support.) During those three days, Grandpa took care of a lot of unfinished business. He made peace with Melissa, his daughter, asking her forgiveness for past offenses. He also gave last words of advice and affection to everyone. And for the last time, he gave a huge hug to his grandson Jeffrey.

As they walked out of the room the day Grandpa died, Jeffrey winked at his mom and said, "Mom, Grandpa came back to life because I prayed for him, and I knew he wasn't going to die quite yet."

Because a nine-year-old listened to God, this family is still experiencing a ripple of blessings. Jeffrey's mom experienced significant emotional healing as a result of her conversation with her father, and two other family members reconciled as a result of seeing God work.

Though children are younger and smaller than adults, they don't have a junior version of the Holy Spirit. If you're a child and you've invited Jesus into your life, the same Spirit that speaks to adults can and will speak to you and guide you. And if you're an adult, be alert for the prayer lessons God wants to teach you through each person in your family, including your younger children. Welcome them into the prayer circle and learn together because He sends His messengers in all shapes and sizes.

DISCUSSION OPENERS

1. What prayer lessons have you learned from others, especially from other family members?

2. Look at the Scriptures below that describe how the young shepherd boy David opposed the giant Goliath and how Gideon's small army defeated the Midianites. What can we learn from them?

3. What's the most miraculous thing you've seen God do as a result of prayer? How did that affect your life? your relationship with God? your relationship with others?

SCRIPTURES FOR GOING DEEPER

Judges 7
1 Samuel 17

A PRAYER

Heavenly Father, grant us the kind of childlike faith
that believes nothing is impossible for You and for those who believe in You.
Renew our hearts and teach us to listen to You and to trust You,
abandoning our own understanding and asking You for miracles.
May You bring life anew to the situations we leave in Your able hands.
In Jesus' name, amen.

A PARTING THOUGHT

"Prayer is a mighty force that moves heaven and pours untold treasures of good on earth."

E. M. BOUNDS

Notes

DADDY LOVES ME

1. Bill Brown, president of Bryan College, communicated this story to me through e-mail.

2. Jean-Nicholas Grou, *How to Pray*. Excerpted in Richard Foster and James Bryan Smith, ed., *Devotional Classics: Selected Readings for Individuals and Groups* (New York: HarperSanFrancisco, 1993), 140.

FAITH THAT MOVES A MOUNTAIN

1. My thanks to Dave Spurdle for sharing this story with me.

MR. LUMP

1. For more of Michael's heartwarming story, see the book his dad, Jeff Leeland, wrote called *One Small Sparrow* (Sisters, Ore.: Multnomah, 1996).

PRAYER CHORUS

1. E. M. Bounds, *Power of Prayer* (Chicago: Moody Press, n.d.), 83. Quoted in Richard Foster, *Celebration of Discipline* (New York: HarperCollins, 1978, 1988), 45.

2. Adapted from booklet titled *Public Schools Power Prayers* by Judy Turpen (Pasadena, Calif: Christian Educators Assn. International, n.d.), 20–1.

LORD, SAVE ME!

1. Story adapted from Matthew 14:22–33.

PRAYING FOR YOUR ENEMIES

1. From "The Inexplicable Prayers of Ruby Bridges" by Robert Coles, *Finding God at Harvard,* Kelly Monroe, ed. (Grand Rapids, Mich.: Zondervan Publishing House, 1996), 33 ff. © Kelly Monroe.

2. From *Current Thoughts and Trends* (9 March 1999), 15. Quoted in *Christian Ministry* (Jan/Feb 1999), 7.

THE STREET WHERE YOU LIVE

1. Corrie ten Boom, *In My Father's House* (Grand Rapids: Mich.: Fleming H. Revell, 1976), 23–4.

2. Ibid., 25.

FRIDAY: PRAYING FOR FAMILY

1. E. M. Bounds, *The Possibilities of Prayer* (Springdale, Penn.: Whitaker House, 1994), 114.

WHEN GOD SAYS WAIT

1. Catherine Marshall, *Adventures in Prayer* (Old Tappan, N.J.: Fleming Revell, 1975), 42–3.

THE STONE BEARERS

1. Larry Crabb, *The Silence of Adam* (Grand Rapids, Mich.: Zondervan, 1995), 56.

HOW DO YOU EXPLAIN GOD?

1. I am indebted to my friend Melanie Hemry who sent me this story via e-mail.

MIGHTY PRAYER PARTNERS

1. Story adapted from Exodus 17:8–13.

2. Adapted from *Not Good if Detached* by Corrie ten Boom (Grand Rapids, Mich.: Fleming H. Revell, a division of Baker Book House, 1957). Used in *One Holy Passion*, compiled by Judith Couchman, (Colorado Springs, Colo.: Waterbrook Press, 1998).

GOD WANTS TO USE CHILDREN

1. From an interview with David Walters of Good News Ministries.

2. This story is adapted from my book *When Children Pray* (Sisters, Ore.: Multnomah Publishers, 1998).

THE GRATEFUL LEPER

1. Story adapted from Luke 17:11–19.

PARDON FOR TRAITORS

1. Peter J. Marshall Jr. and David B. Manuel Jr., *The Light and the Glory* (Grand Rapids, Mich.: Fleming H. Revell, 1977), 323–4.

2. Mother Teresa, *No Greater Love,* Becky Benenate and Joseph Durepos, ed. (Novato, Calif.: New World Library, 1997), 110.

PUTTING ON GOD'S ARMOR

1. Jennifer Dean, *The Praying Life* (Birmingham, Ala.: New Hope, 1993), 92.

GOD HEARS US

1. Irina Ratusinskaya, *In the Beginning,* trans. Alyona Kojevnikov (London: Hodder and Stroughton, 1990), adapted in Charles Colson and Ellen Vaughn, *The Body* (Nashville: Thomas Nelson, 1992), 80.

LISTENING TO GOD, PART ONE

1. Story adapted from Acts 9:1–22.

2. Sören Kierkegaard, *Christian Discourses,* trans. Walter Lowie (Oxford: Oxford University Press, 1940), 324, quoted in Richard J. Foster, *Celebration of Discipline* (New York: HarperCollins, 1988), 39.

LISTENING TO GOD, PART TWO

1. Henri Nouwen, *Making All Things New,* excerpted in *Devotional Classics,* Richard J. Foster and James Bryan Smith, eds., (New York: HarperSanFrancisco, 1993), 95.

WHEN THE LORD SAYS PRAY!

1. Adapted from John C.Wilke, M.D., *Life Issues* (15 February 1999 broadcast, transcript number 1986), 1–2.

2. 1 Samuel 3:9.

3. Adapted from the brochure "7 Ways to Pray for Your Missionary" by Bill Wilson (Littleton, Colo.: OMF International, n.d.).

About the Author

Cheri Fuller is a dynamic inspirational speaker and author of a dozen books—one of which won the Gold Medallion Award in 1998—on issues relating to children, women, the family, and learning. She leads a local college Moms In Touch group and is coordinator of a children's prayer group at her church.

Cheri is a contributing editor for *Today's Christian Woman,* and her articles regularly appear in *Focus on the Family, Family Circle, ParentLife,* and other magazines. She is a frequent guest on Focus on the Family, Moody Network's Midday Connection, Prime Time America, and hundreds of radio stations across the country. A former teacher, she loves inspiring others as she speaks at women's retreats and conferences.

Cheri and her husband, Holmes, have three grown children and a granddaughter, and they live in Oklahoma City, Oklahoma. If you would like to contact Cheri for speaking engagements, write or call her at:

P.O. Box 770493
Oklahoma City, OK 73177
Fax: (405) 749-1381
E-mail: cheri@cander.net
Website: www.CheriFuller.com